7
HIGHWAYS
of the
SOUL

APPROBATIONS FOR
7 HIGHWAYS OF THE SOUL

Norman (Nissim) David Levy, a descendant from illustrious families, Nissim Levy and David Beyda. Norman has zeroed in on our American Sephardic Syrian community whom my grandfather Chief Rabbi Jacob Shaul Kassin, and my father Chief Rabbi Shaul Rahamim Kassin being responsible for creating a symbiotic community for the past 100 years. Our community, deeply rooted in "Middle of the Road" known as The Kings Highway, bringing all from right to left into the center, where one feels connected in a serene and calm environment as one unit. We are all descendants from our forefathers and mothers. Abraham, Isaac, Jacob, Sarah, Rivkah, Leah and Rachel keeping our tradition, culture and above all our cherished gift from Hashem to the Jewish nation our Holy Torah (Bible). We reject nobody, and all find warmth and protection under one Talet (Holy Shawl). Norman crystallized the importance of Integrity, Unity, Challenges, Pure Mind, Honesty, Renewed Energy, Humility, and of course, our secret weapon, our Women of Valor, who control our continuity and destiny. Every Jew has a spark of light in their DNA. I have personally reviewed all of Norman's tireless and devoted works, together with him and his commitment to our community. His works and compilations will traverse the Globe.

 Warmly, with High Esteem-

Jacob Israel Shaul Kassin

***

7 Highways of the Soul is a delightful read. Reflections and insights of a person who invested and continues to invest thoughtfully in all he does, the experiences and the takeaways. It can and should be read from beginning to end and then can be referenced repeatedly for inspiration and guidance.

Rabbi Ricky Cohen

***

I have read some of the writings of my good friend Norman D. Levy and am very pleased by the fruits of his labor. This book is sound advice for any parent looking to build and further their relationship with their children. Much of this advice and guidance is rooted in our Holy Torah and will no doubt give direction and clarity to the reader. May Hashem bless Mr. Norman D. Levy to continue to thrive and succeed in much Torah wisdom and spread his advice to the nation of Israel.

Rabbi Moshe Malka (Rabbi / Ohel Yaacob Congregation)

***

"Ask your father and he will relate it to you, your elders and they will tell it to you." (Devarim/Ha'azinu 32:7) The advice a father gives to his son is a treasure of wisdom. The experience of someone who has been through the struggles and tests of this beautiful world are as valuable as they are numerous, and as much as we constantly pray not to be tested, we always need to be ready for the test when it does arrive. Friendly advice from someone who has been there and done that, is priceless. The Path of the Just writes that life is like a complicated maze that only can be completed successfully with the guidance of those who have already gone through it, already knowing where the tricks lie in wait to make you falter and fumble. *7 Highways of the Soul* is written by my very good friend Norman D. Levy. It is a Torah based handbook filled with advice from a father to his children, through guidance and preparation for the journey ahead. An arduous situation can't be completed without the guidance of one's forebears. Although I have not yet read it cover to cover, I have seen many pieces in this beautiful work, and I am excited to see it finally go into print after witnessing firsthand the tremendous care and dedication that Norman has expended in perfecting this valuable compendium of fatherly wisdom. He is a man with sterling character traits coupled with uniquely honest and pure intentions. With this may Hashem let him merit to see the fruits of his labor and Nachat (comfort) from all his descendants for many years to come.

Sincerely,

Rabbi Joey Sultan (Rabbi/Deal Learning Program)

***

Norman wrote a book originally intended to provide valuable life lessons to his children. Of course, those lessons would be applicable to other children and other families. He then self-edited the text and gave it a more universal perspective. Norman has shown us that we don't have to go through trying times to look to grow and become closer to Hashem. Once we recognize His Hand in all that we do and all that happens to us, the sooner we can get more joy and serenity out of life. I have read the transcripts several times and I have learned many valuable lessons that I plan on adopting in my own life. His use of Tanach and other Holy writings as his sources makes this book even that more inspiring. May Hashem continue to shine His Countenance upon him, and may Norman continue to be a positive influence on his children, his grandchildren and all who know and love him.

Max Anteby

***

Dear Norman,

After reading this collection of letters, I'm proud to be considered one of your childhood friends that you continue to refer to! Your "letters" are well thought through and inspiring. I'm sure your children have benefited a great deal from the thoughts. By allowing these letters to be published, the general public will surely find this collection of great value as well.

Your friend,

Gabe Zeitouni

***

It is my privilege to endorse Norman Levy's *7 Highways of the Soul.* I have known Norman for more than 15 years and I've had the good fortune to witness a great deal of Norman's spiritual journey. Norman's words are so honest, and so authentic that the words jump off their pages and into our hearts. I recommend this book to anyone, young and old, who is in search of greater spiritual connection, and insight into the search for greater spirituality in our modern times. Great job, Norman, I look forward to witnessing your continuing spiritual journey for many years to come.

Phil Schwartz

***

It is an honor and a privilege to call Norman my dear friend. Norman's life and guidance told through the stories in this book is an inspiration to us all. This book should be kept close by and read to your children and grandchildren to illuminate the road to leading a more meaningful life. I am proud to be your friend.

David J. Beyda (President Sephardic Bikur Holim)

***

I am enjoying reading these great thoughts from my good friend Norman D. Levy. Norman went through a lot of trials and tribulations in his life. He was able to rise above them because he had the right attitude and the proper hashkafa (perspective) throughout. In this book he shares this outlook with us by applying them through the different stages of his life. "Who is the wise man? One who learns from all." (Ethics of the Fathers 4:1) Norman learned lessons from all his life experiences and applied them to improve himself every step of the way. Thank you for sharing this with us in this book.

Norman, keep up the great work, keep smiling and most important keep making everyone else around you smile. Tizku leshanim rabot. (To remember for many years to come.)

Norman's good friend (Anonymous)

***

I really enjoyed reading Norman D. Levy's book. I highly recommend it to everyone. I've been friends with Norman since he was 3 years old. This book recaptures and describes so many great stories and lessons he's learned over a lifetime facing many challenges. He learned how to overcome those challenges through the life lessons he writes in this book. There's no better way to teach someone than through real life experiences. Norman has had plenty but it's because of those experiences that Norman can illustrate and share with the reader his wisdom and methods on how to persevere through challenging times to enjoy and create good times and memories to cherish forever.

Sammy J. Sutton

***

*7 **Highways of the Soul*** is a guide for you and your children that should always be kept at arm's reach. Where life did not provide us with an instruction booklet, Norman D. Levy took it as a call to action and provided the world with this invaluable guide which is a meticulous compilation of his real-life challenges and how he found the strength to conquer them.

Ike Escava

***

7
HIGHWAYS
of the
SOUL

"And You Shall Teach Your Children"
– Deuteronomy/Ekev 11:19

NORMAN D. LEVY

BIG MOOSE
PUBLISHING

ISBN: 978-1-989840-38-2 (hard cover)
ISBN: 978-1-989840-40-5 (soft cover)
ISBN: 978-1-989840-39-9 (e-book)

Big Moose Publishing 11/2022

This book is dedicated in loving memory to my dear father David Nissim Levy.

A picture of me as a boy with my father.

TABLE OF CONTENTS

(Chapter Name followed by topic of subject content in parentheses)

A letter my father wrote to me when I graduated Magen David Yeshivah Elementary School, June 14, 1979.

7 Highways of the Soul

#1 In Transit:

There are times in our lives when we find ourselves in a life-changing situation. These situations can interrupt our comfort and daily routines. At this point, we are put into "exile" status and are In Transit. The decisions we make at this juncture will impact the next chapter of our lives. Connecting to a healthy environment will prevent us from breathing in the toxic fumes of the highways. Things may seem dark, but faith in Hashem and introspection assists us in choosing The Right Track.

#2 The Right Track:

The road we travel is one of the most important decisions we can make. When we know we are in the right place, we become more confident of a secure setting that will lead us to our goals. Still there are times when a person chooses the wrong track and crosses a different bridge. He should never lose hope since Hashem is always accepting one's return to Him. All he needs to do is to make a U-Turn into his arms. Learning and connecting to Hashem through prayer and following His direction will assist us when we Turn the Corner.

#3 Turning the Corner:
While on The Right Track, there will be a fork in the road. Which way we turn will affect our outcome. With a newly developed confidence in ourselves and faith in Hashem's guidance, we can trust our internal compass to choose the correct highway for us. If we choose the wrong road, we can always make a U-Turn. When we make the correct turn, it's then time to Stay the Course.

#4 Staying the Course:

It can be rough terrain on this highway. Potholes and confusing byways can test our faith in Hashem and ourselves. It can be a long boring road and we might fall asleep at the wheel. Awareness and patience are some of the most important factors on this road. It's a continued investment in ourselves to ensure we are Following the Signs.

#5 Following the Signs:

It is important to pay attention to the roadmap signs sent to us by Hashem. It is His way of communicating to us and telling us that we are on our way to our destination. All we must do is pay the toll and Cross the Bridge.

#6 Crossing the Bridge:

Once we make this decision, we rarely turn back. It's time to leave the past behind and move forward. We are now in a new place in our lives. It's a new world for us and we should be thankful to Hashem that we are very close to being Home once again.

#7 Home Sweet Home:

After a long trip from what may feel like an extended exile, we are finally back Home and life becomes a do over. Our routines are set. Once home, our renewed and strengthened faith in Hashem and His commandments will serve as a legacy to our future generations.

Our nation has been in exile for close to 2,000 years. Thankfully, our ancestors chose The Right Track, Turned the Corners correctly, Stayed the Course and Followed the Signs on how to live our lives. All we must do is pray to Hashem to redeem us and send the Messiah to Cross the Bridge into Jerusalem, our Home Sweet Home.

INTRODUCTION

ONE MAN/ONE HEART

In the Hebrew year 2448 (1312 BCE), our nation stood at Mount Sinai to receive the Torah. At Sinai, we were 3 million people as "One Man/One Heart." Three thousand years later, our Syrian Community is living the same way. Our community has been blessed due to our love for one another. When one person is in pain, we are all in pain. When we celebrate, we celebrate together. The Synagogues, Yeshivas, and institutions are foundations for the next generation.

With G-d's blessing, I was fortunate enough to be born into this community with rich traditions. Our fathers and grandfathers sacrificed their lives to make sure we had stability. In 1933, Rabbi Jacob S. Kassin arrived from Israel to lead our community. He led us for 60 years. He established the fabric that made our community unique and special. Our respect for our leaders and Rabbis unifies our community to this day and hopefully forever.

I was born on April 7, 1965. I was blessed with parents that sacrificed their lives for me and my three younger sisters. My mother was always there and often opened her home to celebrate holidays with our family and extended families. Spending time with family kept us close and unified.

I got married at the age of 20 and I had my first three children between the ages of 21- 28. My dad and I were in the retail business and were very successful. Our religious traditions were always part of my soul. I prayed every day and was always connected to Hashem (the Almighty), in my own way. However, when I was 28 years old, the business model changed, and business declined. We lost our leases. It was a very difficult time for me both financially and emotionally. Overnight, I went from an employer to an employee, and it was challenging to climb back up the ladder of success. For the first time in my life, my confidence was compromised.

At the age of 34, I had to start over again and adjust to some major life transitions. The loss of my business ultimately led to challenges in all areas in my life. My marriage was dissolved, and I had to move on. At this time, I found myself In Transit (the first highway of the soul).

During those challenging times, I found my comfort in writing articles for the Jewish Image Magazine. The articles were an outlet to how I was feeling, and I hoped it would serve as inspiration to others. Writing became an outlet for me to find The Right Track (the second highway of the soul).

From 2000-2015, I wrote over 100 articles. In the meantime, I had choices to make regarding the next chapter in my life. The choice was whether to leave the community and start a new life in California or stay and deal with the cards dealt to me. It was an easy decision. When I looked into my children's eyes, I said to myself, "If I fall, they will fall." That was not an option for me. I knew I needed to stay. I Turned the Corner (the third highway of the soul) and knew the direction I must take.

At 38 years old, my close friend and cousin suggested that I start learning and going to synagogue every morning. I listened to him. I chose to Stay the Course (the fourth highway of the soul).

That decision set the stage for me to connect with Hashem and my childhood friends. There were lots of challenges, but through my writing and connecting to Hashem I was able to get through the dark tunnel and get to my destination. Establishing a new life with Torah, faith, and in a wonderful community, I was able to start my life over at 47. I Followed the Signs (the fifth highway of the soul) Hashem sent me and I met a wonderful woman who is now my wife and we have been blessed with two children.

My main influence to create this book occurred in 2017. My wife and I moved to New Jersey, and I needed to occupy my time while I was commuting everyday. I decided to reread the articles I wrote for Jewish Image Magazine again to find out where I was in my life at the time I wrote them. From this, I decided to use these articles as a way to impart a gift to my children. I had Crossed the Bridge (the sixth highway of the soul) and was ready to pass this advice onto my children.

The best gift we can give our children is advice. The advice I am giving is from life experience and teaching that life does not always go as planned. We will be dealt situations to test our faith in Hashem and strengthen our resilience to life's tribulations. More than money, success, and power, children need to know the importance of community, friends, family, and most of all a connection to Hashem. Despite a rocky road, I am grateful I am finding my way Home Sweet Home (the seventh highway of the soul.)

I hope and I pray that we continue to live as a community as "One Man/One Heart." Unity among family members, community members, and as a nation will bring about the final redemption. Amen.

OVERVIEW

From the many articles I wrote over the years for Jewish Image Magazine, some key points emerged. Below is an overview of the main themes addressed throughout this book. I truly believe that if one follows these points, they will find peace and joy in life, and it will make navigating the highway of your life easier.

If you're in a hurry, and just need a quick reminder to keep you on track, skim through this list and see what draws you in. Alternatively you can look in the Table of Contents and see what topic calls to you or catches your eye, turn to that page, and see what message is there for you.

Overcome Adversaries: Adversaries are sent to us by Hashem to strengthen us to become more resilient.

Importance of Family Harmony: Family is the best support system we are blessed with. To ensure a close-knit family, treat all family members with respect, love, and support.

Gift of Shabbat: Shabbat is a special day to reconnect with Hashem as well as our families and friends. It's a reconnecting device to gear us up for the following week. The greatest prescription for peace of mind is the gift of the Shabbat. Shabbat is a day to cease all mundane activities and appreciate the beautiful world the creator has designed for us.

Find Your True Soulmate: Our soulmates are predetermined by Hashem. However, we must be in the right time and place to be able to merit it. When we are true to ourselves, our soulmate can arrive with the help of Hashem. The most effective means to find our true soulmate is prayer.

Livelihood/Mazal: Each person is created with a special talent designed by Hashem. It is up to each of us to discover that talent and use it for a trade and livelihood. Hashem provides for all. In our profession, we should love what we do. The rest is up to Hashem and our Mazal.

Power of Prayer: Prayer is a connection to Hashem. The power of prayer is our greatest asset to ensure a happy, fulfilled life.

Subdue Anger: Anger is harmful to our mental and physical health. Anger can destroy families, friendships, and businesses. Anger is a lack of faith in Hashem. When we get angry at others, we are indirectly expressing anger at Hashem.

Forgiveness: If we want to be forgiven by Hashem, please forgive others. The power of forgiveness is a tool to receive G-dly influx.

Achieving Independence: We are a free nation and should never be subservient to another person. Confidence in ourselves will help us achieve independence. Faith in Hashem will help us succeed in our lives.

Humility: Once we achieve success, it is okay to feel great inside. However, we must realize it is all from Hashem. Moshe, Abraham, and David thought of themselves as nothing. They knew their greatness inside, but, on the outside, they were humble and knew it came from Hashem. Arrogance is not received well by Hashem.

Overcoming Challenges/Fearlessness: When a person is on the correct path in life, he will overcome challenges with lack of fear. A person of faith and confidence in Hashem's protection will be a winner and fearless in achieving his goals.

Carve Yourself out of Stagnancy (the Robotic Zone): We are created in the image of Hashem. We are created with unlimited potential. We should imitate Hashem's ways by constantly recreating ourselves. Don't let the grass grow under your feet! Don't be lazy! Just keep going and growing.

Sensitivity Towards Inviting One into Your Home: When inviting guests into your home, please be sensitive towards his/her discomfort. Be like Abraham – his home was a free hotel for his guests. Upon receiving guests, provide them with food, drink, and escort them out of the home towards their destination.

The One Most Important Asset Is Your Children: True wealth is our children. They represent our Legacy. At a very young age, train them according to Hashem's way and they will never stray. A student can be considered a child, since you are mentoring them with proper instructions for a fulfilled life.

A State of Happiness Will Bring Prophecy, Inner Peace: It's a commandment to be happy. Being happy demonstrates faith and confidence in Hashem's ways. Our ancestors were able to receive prophecy while being in state of happiness. If you are not feeling great, try to divert your attention to what will make you happy. It's a major ingredient of being Jewish.

Behind the Curtain (Scenes): Hashem is orchestrating your entire life. If we take inventory of our lives, we will undoubtedly realize that it was Hashem working behind the curtain, shielding, always saving and protecting us.

Community: Be thankful to live in our wonderful community. We are blessed and the one community that is unique.

The Shield Is Our Edict; It's Our No Fly Zone: Chief Rabbi Jacob S. Kassin[ZT"L] enforced an edict in 1935 to keep us a separated insulated community. The perception of our Rabbi saved our community. If not for the edict, our community would have been lost. It is our greatest shield. We all know where we should and shouldn't be. We all know where we can fly and where we can't.

Avoid Addictions: One's internal enemy is the urge to gamble, drink, or do drugs. Be careful of artificial atmospheres that can stimulate your system to want to engage in drugs, gambling, immorality, etc. You must create a fence around it, with a healthy atmosphere of friends and family. We have an obligation to watch our souls. Avoiding addiction safeguards our bodies and souls.

Tehilim Is the Best Musical Prayer to Hashem: Tehilim is our trademark of prayer. When King Saul was upset, King David would play the harp for him. Tehilim is read for all types of needs. It cures the sick and heals one's mind.

The Helper Opposite Him: Man's partner for life is his significant other. She must be set up on a pedestal. Appreciate your wife. She is sent to you by Hashem to help you achieve greatness. A wife is the apparatus to one's health, wealth, and success. Appreciate how a wife selflessly, tirelessly cares for the children.

When I moved to New Jersey, I looked up and saw this message: "Norman D In Transit".

PART 1

THE FIRST HIGHWAY OF THE SOUL: IN TRANSIT

June 1999 - March 2003

There are times in our lives when life throws us a curveball. Between June of 1999 and March of 2003, my life became very unstable. I am a person that is very strict with routine. At this time, routine had to take a backseat to adjusting to a new lifestyle. The life transition of adjusting to no longer being married, finding the right career opportunity, and taking kids on weekends was overwhelming. My mother and friends were always there to assist me with the kids but, unfortunately, I was drifting from religion and was looking outside the community to start a new future. I never missed a day of prayer, even though my head wasn't there. The community lifestyle, Shabbat, and concentrating on my children maintained my focus which was to do my best to set an example for them. This is where writing became my therapy. Every month, the Jewish Image Magazine would publish an article I wrote. The letters that follow are all from those articles. During these times, I was In Transit, not knowing if I would find the right road towards my goals. Still, I had faith that Hashem would lead me out of the darkness and uncertainty.

THE SILVER LINING

"With prayer and closeness to Hashem, you can turn a tragedy into a triumph."

My Dear Children,

Despite the challenges you may face in your lifetime, you have a responsibility to set a good example for your children. It's easy to walk away from a difficult situation, but an honorable man will depend on his integrity and his faith by confronting all situations in a responsible way. You may be angry or bitter at times. Using the values you've been taught will make you a better man/woman, when facing life's thresholds, and it is most rewarding. You will never understand the reason Hashem introduces tragedy into one's life[1]; however, if you try to do the right thing in every situation, you will be setting a beautiful example for your children. Hopefully by witnessing your actions, they too will become honest, respectable people who do what's right and depend on G-d. Always look for "The Silver Lining" in every cloud; it is always there. The way we react is the way our children will act.

Love, Daddy

DIVIDE AND CONQUER
"Relationships should have borderlines that must not be crossed."

My Dear Children,

It is important to surround yourself with loving people. Those who truly have your best interests at heart will never try to control you. They will never criticize you with the sole intention of making you feel bad or inferior. However, there are times when a friend, acquaintance, or even a family member may want to control you. This could be a result of a personal insecurity or a quest to fill something missing in his life. He may do it to gain recognition or approval. You are human and allowed to make mistakes. When you are criticized, please check where it is coming from. Someone who loves you may offer constructive criticism to help you. Criticism from one who does not have your best interest at heart is not healthy. It can affect your confidence and rob you of your self-worth; thus, it is important to set up borders in any relationship you are in.[2] Never give anyone ammunition to hurt you. Choose your friends and people you confide in very carefully. It doesn't pay to fight with controlling people, because they are only putting you down to lift themselves up. Please pray to Hashem to protect you, always be confident in yourself, with humility, and remember that every relationship must have limitations that shouldn't be crossed, by using the "Divide and Conquer" rule.

Love, Daddy

HEARTS AND SOULS

"We must build our own sanctuary of confidence in ourselves."

My Dear Children,

At some point in your life, you may experience a challenge in a relationship or a job situation that drains you mentally and physically. Let's call it a discomfort zone. This, unfortunately, can cause a blockage in spiritual growth. Often, this is the result of an aversion to change, coupled with laziness. If you allow this to happen, it can cause an obstruction in your relationship with Hashem. During a challenge, my best advice is to take it one day at a time. Choose to be around friends and family who can offer advice and who have your best interests at heart. Don't let anything come between you and Hashem. His spirit hovers over you. It is up to you to find Him, and invite Him to dwell inside of you, in your own inner sanctuary.[3] Please have faith that He has sent you this discomfort to help you grow. Please choose a Rabbi or a mentor and humbly ask for help. Know that these individuals can guide you out of your discomfort and help you maintain a healthy "Heart and Soul."

Love, Daddy

MIXED MESSAGES

"Hashem always gives us the opportunity to return to Him."

My Dear Children,

When life becomes difficult and things are not working out the way you planned, it can cause negative physical and emotional effects, which can make you bitter. Unfortunately, when this happens, many people turn to drugs and alcohol to make themselves feel better. And it may seem to work, but only for a moment. It's very dangerous. These vices will only make matters worse. Instead of turning to drugs, turn to Hashem. Please, try to remember that challenges are opportunities sent by Hashem to make you a better person. Try to accept them with faith, pray for help, maintain a positive attitude, and despite all that is going wrong, try to smile. A simple smile can make you feel better and bring those who have become distant back into your life. You are beautiful; just take things one day at a time. Please don't let the confusion of "Mixed Messages" dictate your decisions. Hashem is always there to forgive and assist you.[4]

Love, Daddy

WHEELS IN MOTION

"Life is constantly in motion; there is little time to be complacent."

My Dear Children,

If you are working hard at your career and relationships, taking a break from work, going on vacation, and relaxing are wonderful. We don't want you to get lazy, preferring comfort to work. It's easy to become complacent, especially when things are going well. However, please don't take anything for granted. Try to make life better by planning your next move[5], whether it's working towards a promotion or making sure your spouse knows that he/she is appreciated. In your growth, please never let the grass grow under your feet. Have passions and dreams. Keep striving towards that next goal, thus keeping the "Wheels in Motion," and you will be incredibly successful.

Love, Daddy

BROTHERLY LOVE
"Self esteem is one of the building blocks of success."

My Dear Children,

When you receive criticism, take note from who it comes – because there are two types of criticism and two types of people. Constructive criticism comes from people who truly want to help you succeed. Nonconstructive criticism comes from insecure people who want to sabotage your progress, usually because they're jealous of your accomplishments. That's why it's so important to surround yourself with people who love and admire you. There may be times when you think someone has your best interests at heart, yet he/she puts you down in little ways, making you feel insecure. This person may be trying to control you. If you start to believe the things he/she says, you can find yourself in a downward spiral to a dark place. It's okay to consider whether the things this person is saying are true. It's healthy to be introspective and question your intentions now and then. However, if you know you're on the right path, you must accept that this person is toxic, and you must eliminate him/her from your life. My strongest advice is do not give anyone the power to control who and what you are. If you have questions, seek advice from mentors. And never be the person giving nonconstructive criticism. Always accentuate the positive and use your G-d given talents and the values you were taught to give positive advice, and try to bring about "Brotherly Love" and unity.[6]

Love, Daddy

GROUND ZERO

"Ground Zero is an opportune time for introspection."

My Dear Children,

While living a secure, happy existence, sometimes life throws a curve ball, a game changer that can alter your daily routine. It could be a job change, a divorce, or anything that disrupts your daily life. The way you react to such a situation will determine the outcome. This is the time when you must have faith in Hashem and surround yourself with loving, understanding people. Try to continue doing the things that are important to you. Develop a set time for prayer, exercise, and anything that makes you feel productive. Being at ground zero - the central point in a time of fast change or the starting point of a new reality - is scary, but it's also an opportunity for greatness.[7] Try not to wallow in bitterness or self-pity. Ground Zero can be a dark place. The more you dwell on your problems and feel sorry for yourself, the longer it will take to see light out of the darkness. During the transition, try to have patience and stay away from people who will distract you from rebuilding a new normal daily routine that is healthy. Life is a test of faith in Hashem, so have faith, and establish an even better routine. From "Ground Zero" please have faith that Hashem is good, and He sees the big picture.

Love, Daddy

STANDING UP

"One can stand as an observer or take a stand and make a difference."

My Dear Children,

There are times that your confidence may be challenged. You might feel shy or too respectful to stand up for yourself. Sometimes it may just seem easier to back down. Respect is a good reason to let a situation pass; however, there are times when you must stand up for yourself. Allowing anyone to take advantage of you, because you are unable to advocate on your own behalf, can hurt your self-esteem, which can lead to anger, bitterness, and even addiction. I am not saying that you must stand up to everyone who says anything derogatory to you; however, don't let people mistake your kindness for weakness. Most of the time, letting such situations go is the right thing to do. The time to stand up for yourself is when it really matters. It is when someone is invalidating you, or something important to you. In a calm manner, let them know why you disagree, but don't say anything you might regret. Once you stand up to a bully, you'll be happy you did. Standing up for yourself and your beliefs is empowering.[8] Follow your instincts. Know when to take a stand and when to let it go, especially when you can let it go in a way that shows that the person assaulting your self-esteem isn't worth your time. It shows incredible control. It's rewarding and it will keep you "Standing Up" in the right place.

Love, Daddy

ALL'S WELL THAT ENDS WELL

"Each ending is a window for a new beginning."

My Dear Children,

Life can be going great and look very promising; then suddenly, there can be a game changing moment that can affect everything.[9] This is Hashem's way of showing you nothing ever remains the same; it's all part of His bigger picture. Your attitude towards the challenge will dictate your future. It will either help or hinder you. It's okay to feel dismayed for a little while but you must pick yourself up and have faith that all will be well. We don't understand Hashem but have confidence that He will provide healing. Don't let one change alter your optimistic outlook on life. Changes and challenges can bring about all sorts of wonderful new opportunities; you just must recognize them. "All's Well that Ends Well" is dependent on your attitude and faith in Hashem.

Love, Daddy

PART 2
THE SECOND HIGHWAY
OF THE SOUL:
THE RIGHT TRACK

March 2003 - February 2006

In March of 2003, my close friend and cousin drove me home from NYC. He advised me to come to the Synagogue in the morning to learn and pray each morning. I took his advice reluctantly. The next morning, I got to synagogue at 6:20am to learn Talmud. I prayed with a group of old friends and acquaintances from my childhood. I felt like I was back home and the reconnection to religion was natural to me. The reestablishment of routine enabled me to start working on myself to move in the right direction. Now that I had a stable support system, I knew I was on the right road.

My dad was struggling with his health. Part of my routine became to be there for him multiple times a day. I found a career opportunity in sales. After a few years of financial struggle, bills were being paid on time and I established a renewed faith in Hashem. I was on the "Right Track" and was confident that Hashem was guiding and protecting me. The letters that follow are about getting on track and staying there.

MUSICAL ROUTINES
"Daily routines establish structure."

My Dear Children,

Once you have a family of your own, friends, and a daily routine that begins with an expression of gratitude to Hashem, you are well on your way down the path to success. When your routine is disturbed, don't let it discourage you. Once you have a foundation of family and friends who are always there to support you, and a relationship with Hashem, no calamity can cause irreversible damage. Your day should begin with a routine of prayer and expressing gratitude to Hashem. The most effective tool is to maintain a solid faith in the big picture of Hashem's plan. This will maintain your balance through the routine of change. "Musical Routines" of faith and prayer will help you connect to Hashem.[10]

Love, Daddy

SELFISHLY SELFLESS

"Man must create for himself a universe others will benefit by."

My Dear Children,

Being a leader, someone who wants to help the people who look up to him/her, is complicated. A good leader wants to help others attain their goals and gives of himself expecting nothing in return.[11] He should not do it for accolades of any kind. That sounds simple enough, however, one should not give so much that it drains him financially or emotionally. A great leader knows exactly how much he can give, when to give it and how. He assists others not to feed his ego, but to emulate Hashem. Never stop helping others, but please make sure it is done for the right reasons, and don't give more than you can afford to give. In order to protect yourself, it is okay to be "Selfishly Selfless."

Love, Daddy

LOVING KINDNESS
"Demonstrating kindness will bring you peace and long life."

My Dear Children,

I've enjoyed watching you grow as individuals and as siblings. You have kept close to each other in challenging times. I hope that you continue to rely on each other, as you enter adulthood and beyond. Please continue to be there for each other emotionally and financially, offering support when needed. There will be times when you don't agree, but don't sweat the petty little stuff. And if there is ever "big stuff," try to put your egos aside and find a compromise – even if you agree to disagree. No matter what, at the end of the day, you're family. Be good to each other. Always give of yourself to your family, friends, and community.[12] "Loving Kindness" is a great mitzvah. May G-d shower blessings upon you. Amen!

Love, Daddy

CONFIDENTLY MIRACULOUS

"Accountability results in higher self-esteem."

My Dear Children,

If you're lucky, when you're a child, everything is done for you, given to you, and beyond doing well in school, you have little to worry about. Mommy and Daddy take care of everything. There will come a time when you have to make important decisions that will impact your future. The key is to remain steadfast in your beliefs, be honest, and have faith in G-d.[13] I pray that Mom and I will be here for a long time to offer support and advice when you ask for it. We want you to be confident in your own decisions. We also want you to know that we are here for you. If you ever find yourself struggling for any reason, let us know. We will always do all we can for you. In addition, there are two things you should keep in mind. The first, if something doesn't feel right, 99% of the time, it's not right. The second, although your family and friends are here for you, ultimately, the path your life takes is between you and Hashem. With faith you should "Confidently" make the first move and Hashem will perform the "Miraculous" for you.

Love, Daddy

SEEING IS BELIEVING

"Once one believes that Hashem is a partner in his life, his eyes will open up and see the inner beauty of the universe."

My Dear Children,

If you ever have a difficult time and feel challenged, please remember that you are never alone. Hashem is with you and will heal all your wounds. He created you with a specific purpose and will challenge you to make yourself a better, stronger person. There may come a time when your faith wanes. You may question why you should believe in G-d when you can't see Him. If this happens, pray for help, and look for signs in your everyday life that He hears you. In the meantime, stay close to positive people. Create a routine that you enjoy and take life day by day. Once you "See" G-d's loving hand supporting you, it will cause you to "Believe" that you will be carried towards a better place in your life.[14]

Love, Daddy

WITHOUT A DOUBT

"A proper support system helps one eliminate self-doubt."

My Dear Children,

There are going to be times that you might question yourself about a decision you made. Sometimes it will be the wrong decision for that time, but due to self-doubt you might dwell in that place. It could be a relationship, job, or friendship that drained you emotionally. The best advice I can give you is once something drains you, design an exit plan. It is your gut telling you that it's not right. It is Hashem talking to you and telling you it is time to move on to better things. After you leave that area of your life, the last thing you can do is regret it. Please put your faith in Hashem, that He is there, and never doubt His love for you. Self-doubt is a lack of confidence and a spiritual Amalek.[15] You must eradicate it and get it out of your system by believing in yourself and "Without a Doubt" stop second guessing yourself.

Love, Daddy

REVIVING HEARTS

"Assisting others helps them regain hope for a successful future."

My Dear Children,

During life, you may feel alone and in a dark place. It is dark there, but you have a choice on how to handle it. Helping others that have fallen, visiting the sick and having healthy relationships with friends and family will assist you. The other choice will only bring you deeper into an abyss of loneliness that can have lasting effects. Remember to be close to a Rabbi, mentor, or a friend to help support you as you support others. Especially in success, always help others in any way you can as you will be reviving their spirits.[16] That is imitating Hashem and His attributes. Assisting others is like giving birth to them. A smile, financial help, or taking them to dinner are crucial resurrection keys to "Reviving Hearts."

Love, Daddy

MIRACLES OF THE HEART

"The display of emotions determines one's fate."

My Dear Children,

When confronted with changes and other challenges, always trust your heart and instincts.[17] Instead of immediately doing something impulsive to take care of the situation, think about the long-term effects of your actions. If your instincts tell you to wait and see what happens, follow them. The change that you perceive as harrowing today may be exactly what you need tomorrow. It's easy to praise Hashem in the morning when things look bright. The challenging part is to have faith in the dark times. Faith will teach you that there is no such thing as darkness. It was Hashem sending a test of faith. It is not an easy task, but with the right advice and trusting your heart and instincts, you will succeed. If you find yourself in a challenging situation, instead of trying to change it, ask Hashem to help you through it. From there you will see the hidden miracles and notice the light was always there. It is all about faith coupled with the "Miracles of the Heart."

Love, Daddy

FIT TO BE UNTIED

"Moving forward releases one from the imprisonment of his past."

My Dear Children,

There may be times in your life when you feel stagnant. It may be because of a job that is not fulfilling, or you may want to move to a new home, but for some reason you must stay where you are for a while. When this happens, pray to Hashem for the change you desire. He, alone, knows when that change will come and whether it will be for the best. While you're waiting, do everything in your power to help that change materialize, and surround yourself with a strong support system. Patience is key! No person should ever be confined to himself or another human being.[18] Real freedom is demonstrating faith. It's essential that you know it can take years to become an overnight success, and Hashem is watching and waiting for the right time to set you free from whatever is holding you back. One day He will say, "That's enough," and that day will be the beginning of the rest of your life. Maintaining faith in Hashem is crucial. You are never alone, if you know Hashem is with you. With these tools, you will be "Fit to be Untied."

Love, Daddy

YOUR 6TH SENSE

"Trusting one's gut avoids toxic situations."

My Dear Children,

Never choose a path just because it's convenient. Hashem has granted you the intelligence and instincts to know right from wrong.[19] Follow your gut; don't do anything just because someone else wants you to, especially if you know deep down that what they want is wrong. Sometimes saying no to someone is difficult, but it can still be the right thing to do. You must have the confidence to do so. If you're not sure if what is being asked of you is wrong, follow your instincts. This is true when it comes to relationships as well. Just because someone wants to spend time with you, it doesn't mean he/she is a good person to spend time with. Choose relationships that are healthy, and bring you joy. Sometimes, it's better to be alone than in a harmful relationship – not just when it comes to romance, but in friendships, too. You have free will. Don't allow anyone to steer you wrong. Trust "Your 6th Sense." I know you'll always do what's right.

Love, Daddy

GARMENTS OF THE SOUL

"Our daily activities reflect the garments we provide our souls with."

My Dear Children,

Throughout our lifetimes we meet approximately 80,000 people. Of course, not all of them impact our lives, but a great many of them do. Some people influence us in wonderful ways, helping to build our character. These people don't show up by accident. They are sent by Hashem to help us grow spiritually. Thus, no matter whom you meet, or where you meet them, treat everyone with respect, humility, and gratitude. You may ask, why gratitude? The answer is that we are not entitled to anything in this world, and should be appreciative in all areas of life. Unfortunately, some people will mistake your humility for weakness, and try to take advantage of you. If this happens, it's important to confront him/ her and explain that while you treat everyone well, you still have self-respect and you will not allow anyone to mistreat you. Self-respect is "Garments of the Soul" that should be worn with dignity and gratitude.[20]

Love, Daddy

SPIRITUAL RESILIENCE

"Prayer strengthens one's resilience to challenge."

My Dear Children,

Most people find it easier to heal from a broken bone than from a broken heart. When we break a bone, we know that it will take a while to heal. This is a good lesson. When your heart is broken, you can't expect it to heal overnight. It too takes time. Just believe that Hashem is with you, and he feels your pain. When any situation is so stressful that it feels like it will never get better, pray. G-d is always near those who seek Him.[21] Sometimes a longer recovery is more permanent. Hashem will provide the cure, you just need to be patient. Instead of losing faith, pray more. It's easy to fall into a state of depression and wallow in self-pity. Don't wallow! Use this time to work on yourself and help others with similar problems. As you help them, you'll help yourself. Unquestionable faith builds "Spiritual Resilience."

Love, Daddy

FOUNDATIONS

"In order to survive life's challenges, one must build a foundation beneath him."

My Dear Children,

To have a happy life, you need to have a solid foundation on which to live it. Literally, a foundation is something solid that you build upon, such as the foundation of a house. If you look up its meaning in the dictionary, it says, "involving or possessing physical or mental strength; solid or robust in construction; not easily broken or injured; having a resolute will, or morally firm and incorruptible character; intense in quality." I want all of this for you. Mom and I tried to build a strong foundation for you while you were growing up. And you need to continue building on it every day. With an excellent moral foundation, one can make better decisions. A person without a good foundation is not resilient to life's changes.[22] Every challenge seems like chaos, and one bad decision can affect all areas of life. He/she may decide, G-d forbid, to do drugs to make life go away for a while. DO NOT! With a solid foundation you know better than to make that choice. Be sure to thank Hashem often for your spiritual foundation, which our religion and our community has helped build. Life is constantly changing; with a proper foundation you will be able to pass your "Foundations" of success to future generations.

Love, Daddy

Sense of Direction

"Humility causes Hashem to direct one's steps in the right direction."

My Dear Children,

It's important to realize that you are granted the free will to take any path you choose. However, there will probably be times in your life when you want something but can't figure out how to get it. You may want to purchase a home, send your children to a certain school, or pursue a relationship, yet everywhere you turn, there are blockades stopping you from moving forward. This may be Hashem informing you that what you want may not be right for you. Always realize with humility that Hashem is directing your steps, and please pray to Him to put you on the right path.[23] If something is not meant to be, don't continue your pursuit. Don't force it. Hashem loves you and is doing what's best for you. Sometimes the right path is made of very rough terrain. If you feel lost, please talk to someone you trust or ask a Rabbi for guidance. Perhaps you just need a push from someone with a better "Sense of Direction".

Love, Daddy

HOPE AND STRENGTH

"Hope and trust in Hashem helps us through obstacles."

My Dear Children,

There may be times when you want to take a chance, but find you're afraid. This can be attributed to low self-esteem. This is a good time to turn to members of your support system. Remember, you chose them because they bring out the best in you. Hopefully, they will give you the strength you need to take that chance. And turn to Hashem, because He is merciful and can give you hope and strength. Hopefully, others will turn to you for support when they're feeling overwhelmed.[24] Then, you can encourage them to take a risk, and help build up their self-esteem. Let them know that hope is never lost and every day is a new opportunity to feel better. Helping others will help you receive renewed strength and hope. That's the wonderful thing about helping those you love. When you help them and when they help you, everybody is encouraged, and your relationship grows even deeper with renewed "Hope and Strength.".

Love, Daddy

NECESSARY PROVISIONS

"Hashem's light is going to shine on those with integrity."

My Dear Children,

One of the most challenging experiences in your life may be financial in nature. With the alarming rate of inflation today, it can be difficult to keep up with others, and that's okay; it shall never be your goal. Don't worry about what others have. Please remember that all wealth comes from Hashem. He provides us with all we need, always.[25] Even if you reach a point where you're not saving as much money as you would like, please don't let that stop you from giving charity. If you are unable to give financially, please give in another way. Volunteer your time to assist others. If Hashem sends you lots of wealth, please be disciplined. Don't gamble or be careless with it. Some good advice is to save and put together a monthly budget, and of course, give tzedakah. Don't be impulsive! Constantly thank Hashem for all He has given you. If, on the other hand, you have trouble making ends meet, remember, Hashem always gives you the "Necessary Provisions" and you will always be just fine.

Love, Daddy

DEDICATED IN BELOVED MEMORY OF
OUR REVERED AND ESTEEMED PATRIARCH
AND SPIRITUAL LEADER
CHIEF RABBI JACOB S. KASSIN, A"H, ZT"L
WHO LED, GUIDED AND INSPIRED OUR COMMUNITY
WITH HOLINESS, DIGNITY AND HONOR FOR 64 YEARS
IT IS IN HIS MERIT AND LIFE EXAMPLE OF
EXTRAORDINARY LOVE AND DEVOTION TO HASHEM,
THE TORAH AND HIS PEOPLE
THAT WE ARE STILL BEING BLESSED TODAY
1984/5744
2006/5766
We, the Leaders
Syrian and Near Eastern Sephardic Communities
Reaffirm
1935/5695
1946/5706
A Subsequent Clarification
THE EDICT OF 1935

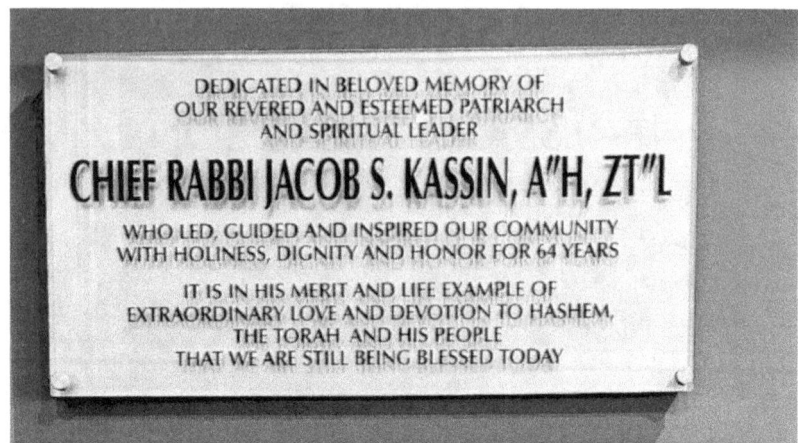

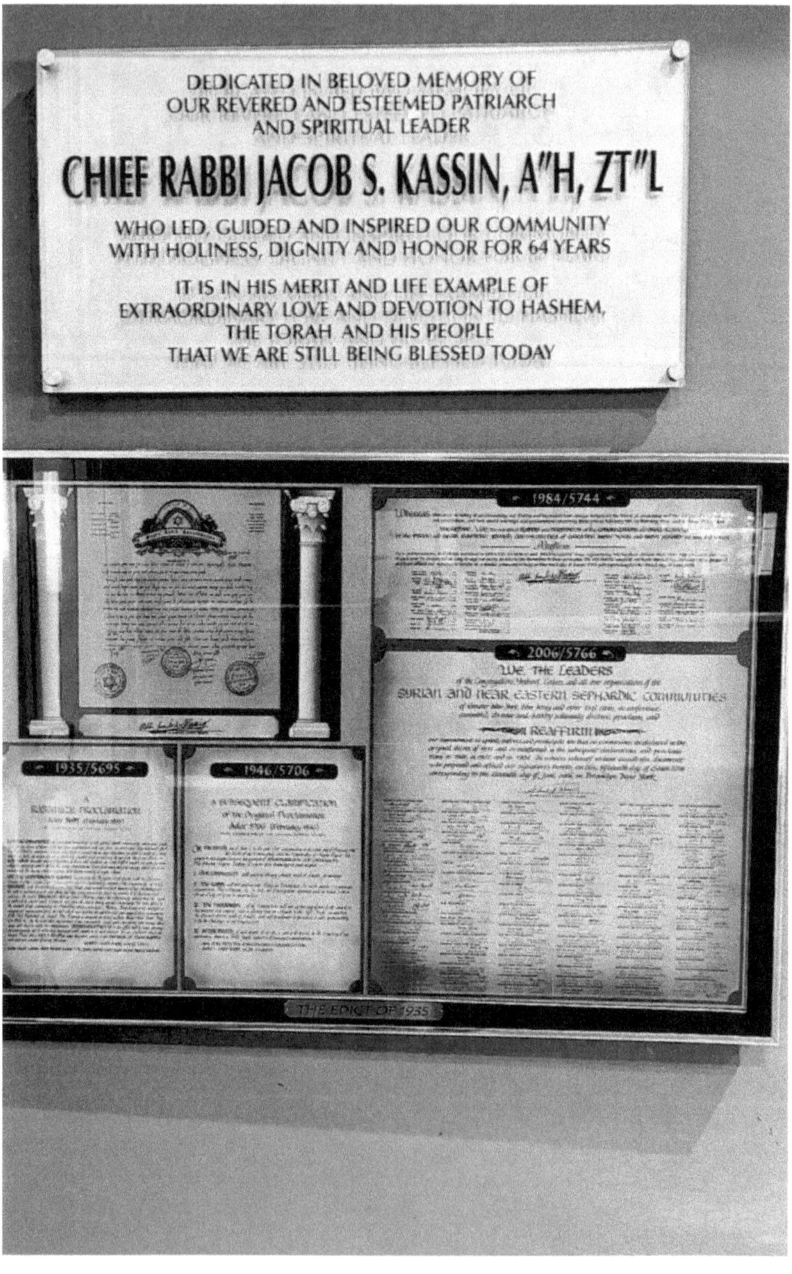

SPIRITUAL WEAPONS

"It is our obligation to recognize Hashem and thank Him for giving us the strength to live each day."

My Dear Children,

Throughout the 2000 year exile of the Jewish people, nations have tried to destroy us. We pray each morning for Hashem to give us the strength to overcome our enemies. We may not see it, but He is fighting our battles all the time. All you must do is connect with Hashem and appreciate His kindness. How many persecutions have we gone through and yet, we are still here? It is Hashem's promise to us that He will never abandon His people.

In life, when you face a battle, always remember that prayer is the best weapon you have.[26] Sometimes the battle will be tough, but the harder the battle, the stronger you will become. The most brutal of enemies is the evil inclination inside of you. Thus, you must have faith in yourself and in Hashem. If you are on the right path, Hashem will always be there for you. If you ever fall off course, please don't condemn yourself, you are human. My best advice is to get back on the path and take it day by day. Don't overwhelm yourself; just be patient. Faith and prayer are the most effective "Spiritual Weapons" against your enemies.

Love, Daddy

SPIRITUAL BEAUTY

"Humility is not having or showing any feelings of superiority."

My Dear Children,

As you proceed on your journey, the material, physical, and superficial world will try to engulf you. Do not allow yourself to be influenced by materialistic people and beautiful things. The best way to make sure it doesn't affect you is to be happy with yourself! You are blessed with a powerful soul, which is so much more important than anything you can buy. Most superficial societies are attention grabbing, insecure groups searching for recognition. You were not brought up in that sort of place. You may be beautiful on the outside but know that your inner beauty and your love of Hashem are your true wealth. Helping others, staying humble, honest, and thanking Hashem for everything is how you express your inner beauty.[27] Family, community, and friends should always be your top priorities. Stay away from people and places that are compromising towards your spiritual growth. Our souls are never for sale because they belong to Hashem. It's up to you to show your "Spiritual Beauty."

Love, Daddy

SPIRITUAL UNIQUENESS

"Each person is required to discover his own uniqueness."

My Dear Children,

The Torah way of life is the only way of life. It provides routine and respect for others, kindness, along with a certain uniqueness, which is part of your DNA. Like Abraham, who used his uniqueness to start a nation, I implore upon you to discover your own individuality and purpose in life.[28] You were born to contribute to society and make the world a better place. As you proceed, please never compromise your uniqueness. It's a tough world, but Hashem will assist you. Self-confidence, along with humility and faith in Hashem, will help you discover your niche – your "Spiritual Uniqueness," which will be your platform for success.

Love, Daddy

HAPPINESS IS...

"True happiness arrives when others benefit from one's kindness."

My Dear Children,

When you're in a good, healthy place in life, surrounded by caring people, you will be in the right frame of mind to receive your true calling from Hashem. This is the time when you realize what your goals in life are and you'll find extra energy to pursue them. The true calling of happiness is a result of constantly growing in a positive environment. Throughout your journey, there will be challenges, because nothing good comes easily. The key is to remain steadfast in your journey. Don't allow anyone to stand in your way. Finding your true calling is discovering the happiness within yourself to pursue your dreams.[29] True "Happiness is" being true to yourself.

Love, Daddy

SPIRITUAL CAPTIVITY

"When one makes a difference is someone's life, his efforts have an everlasting ripple effect."

My Dear Children,

I pray that addiction never finds its way into your life. Addiction is one of the worst types of spiritual captivity. I'm not just talking about drug addiction. Addictions are a gravitational pull to the dark side. One can be addicted to wealth, fame, risky behavior, or being the center of attention. This often happens when he or she has lost confidence in her/himself. It's a form of escape from everyday problems and negative thoughts. Although allowing yourself to surrender to an addiction may be tempting, it's certainly not worth the price. If, G-d forbid, you find yourself in any form of captivity, surrender--not to the addiction--but to Hashem and the help of others. Please connect with a group, a mentor, or a Rabbi for guidance. A person in prison cannot free himself alone. He needs support![30] If you should connect with someone who wants to lead you away from your faith and further into the abyss, don't follow. You be the leader. Try to bring this person, and anyone else who needs help, back onto the right path. If you're able to do this, it will demonstrate to you just how strong you are and build your self-confidence, keeping you out of "Spiritual Captivity."

Love, Daddy

WOMAN OF VALOR

"It is doubtful whether any executive position requires greater skill than domesticating a household."

My Dear Son,

Some people think success comes from the courage to seek and find one's own fortune, however, there are three things that are more important. They are a good wife, faith in Hashem, and hard work. We know you have faith in Hashem, and you will work hard for what you want, so let's focus on a woman of valor. Without a wife to take care of everything at home, a man would have difficulty attaining success. A wife stabilizes and strengthens a man, while encouraging him to achieve his goals. When you find such a woman, be sure to express appreciation and give her a lot of attention. A wife reflects her husband. If she is happy, it is because her husband is making her happy. Unfortunately, the opposite is true as well. If you are critical and controlling, she can become a most challenging adversary instead of your greatest partner. Please treat her well. When you argue, be introspective. Instead of focusing on your disagreement, think about all the things she does for you, and your children, and why you should appreciate her. This will create peace. If you are respectful and attentive to her, you'll be able to solve almost any disagreement. It's about open and honest communication. A "Woman of Valor" is a blessing, the source of future blessings, and behind every successful family.[31]

Love, Daddy

NATURAL BATTERIES

"Studying the miracle of the human body helps us reflect in the wisdom of G-d."

My Dear Children,

Throughout your life, you will face challenges. They come from all areas of our lives including relationships, financial, employment, etc. That's why it's so important to recognize and appreciate the little things in life that bring happiness. They come from Hashem and we should be grateful for them. When we're young, we often think we're invincible and invulnerable to disease. However, G-d forbid, all it takes is a sprained ankle or a small health issue to remind us just how fragile human beings are. The human body is a gift from Hashem.[32] Try not to take it for granted. Treat it well and it will respond well. Being grateful for your health, and other things that we often take for granted, will help when life's challenges come along. Exercise and proper nutrition are essential for recharging our "Natural Batteries," mentally and physically.

Love, Daddy

CELLS IN HEAVEN
"Prayer is a phone call to Hashem."

My Dear Children,

Before cell phones were invented, we would often sit by the phone, all day long, waiting for an important phone call. And without caller ID, we would answer the phone without knowing who was calling. Sometimes it was someone we didn't feel like talking to, and other times just hearing the voice on the other side would make our day. None of that happens anymore. We don't wait for phone calls. We go about our lives, and when the call arrives, we take our smartphones out of our pockets and answer them. We always know who's calling, and often choose not to answer, if we don't feel like talking. The purpose of a phone call is communication. Yet, with the advancement of technology, there is amazingly less person-to-person communication than there was back then. Although we often choose not to answer the phone, Hashem never does. His line is always open. Sometimes it feels like Hashem isn't listening, but please have faith. Hashem takes every call (hears your prayers).[33] Sometimes the answer is no, but He knows when to say yes! It's about faith and patience. So, when someone calls, give him the courtesy of answering. The way we answer others is how we will be answered. Please always be polite and courteous on the phone, text, or email. Your prayers are phone calls to the "Cells in Heaven" and the line is never busy.

Love, Daddy

41

MOUTH TRAPS

"Positive words of praise and encouragement have an everlasting effect."

My Dear Children,

Unfortunately, we all know people who speak negatively about others. They slander and gossip, and are often responsible for broken marriages, relationships, friendships, etc. Slander destroys businesses, families, and sometimes even nations. Please do not speak badly about others or pass along gossip, even if it seems innocent. Hashem is always listening. He hears every word. So, how should you act when someone slanders you? If what they say is true, perhaps it's a message from Hashem that you should refine your character. However, that doesn't relieve the slanderer's responsibility towards you. You should confront him in a gentle way or just ignore him. You may feel like attacking back, but that's not what Hashem wants. Pray to Hashem to help control your mouth, since a mouth can be a weapon that destroys lives.[34] Exercising restraint will help you avoid the "Mouth Traps" of society.

Love, Daddy

PART 3
THE THIRD HIGHWAY
OF THE SOUL:
TURNING THE CORNER

April 2006 - October 2007

While on a journey, there can be many potholes and diversions. As we progress in our lives, the evil inclination gains strength as well. During the time from April 2006 to October 2007, I was growing spiritually. My confidence and inner strength caused me to become more dependent on Hashem. I was learning a lot about myself. However, being single and all my friends being married, I found myself associating with friends that were not on my religious page. It started to confuse me and caused me to question my religious beliefs. It was like living a double life. I was going out at night, and then spending the next morning in Synagogue; this was not the correct way to live a life. Luckily, I was trained by my dad to never take drugs or gamble. I found myself thankful that Hashem didn't send me an abundance of wealth, since it could have ruined me. While "Turning the Corner", I was continuing my growth in Torah learning, writing and religious observance.

When you find your faith waning or are unsure of yourself, may you find support and strength in these next set of letters.

SEEDS IN HEAVEN

"Due to the self-sacrifice of our ancestors, we are recipients of their seeds planted in heaven."

My Dear Children,

Life is a balance sheet. There are times when you will receive a reward, and wonder, What did I do to deserve this? We pray each day in the merit of our forefathers. As a nation, we are still cashing in on the merits of our ancestors.[35] Doing mitzvot and praying is not only about you. Sometimes you may not see your prayer answered in your lifetime, but you should know that it may be held in escrow for future generations. We don't know! I do know that because of our parents/grandparents we are standing here today. They sacrificed their lives for us, and we are recipients of the rewards for their hard work. Sometimes you will see someone unworthy of blessing, flourishing, and wonder why. It is not for us to judge. They probably received that reward from their ancestors. It is all part of G-d's perfect plan. Please continue to pray, as each prayer is a seed and a deposit in Heaven for our legacy. Pray for others; pray for our nation. May your deposits be everlasting "Seeds in Heaven."

Love, Daddy

No Strings Attached

"Selflessly assisting a person in need is a way to emulate Hashem."

My Dear Children,

You are blessed with the very strong, fantastic trait of giving to others. It is very important that you never give anything with strings attached. You are a giver because that is your nature. Hashem blessed you with the gift of giving. It is in the DNA of our religion. Our ancestors did everything for us, not for aggrandizement. Always give unconditionally to others.[36] People who give with conditions are doing it because they want something in return. When you give from your heart without a price tag, you'll feel free and not indebted to anyone, nor will they be indebted to you. Try to watch out for people who give with strings attached, as they are controlling and manipulative. When you give, don't even expect a thank you. Always maintain a "No Strings Attached" approach to others. The best things in life are free!

Love, Daddy

REJUVENATION
"Helping others revives their spirits."

My Dear Children,

As change confronts you and things may seem dysfunctional, remember that Hashem will always rejuvenate you. A situation may cause you distress and things may appear hopeless, but it is Hashem who cures all ills. All things heal in time. A most effective way to feel rejuvenated is to assist others. In the future, Hashem will resurrect the dead. In this life, we can be resurrected from a stressful situation. It can be a health issue, or a healing heart. You must have confidence that resurrection occurs daily. The season of the year shows the cycles of life. Springtime is a time of year to witness the rebirth of nature.[37] The same thing will happen during transition. It may take time. Sometimes you may feel disconnected from Hashem. Please realize that all rejuvenations are not only physical or emotional. A person who returns to Hashem is spiritually resurrected. That is a miracle! Through transition, please have confidence that Hashem will always use the "Rejuvenation" process for you to blossom.

Love, Daddy

FRIENDS

"A good friend is one of the best assets a person can have."

My Dear Children,

One of life's greatest gifts is friendship. Please don't take it for granted. A good friend who loves you and wants to see you grow is a blessing.[38] You should be thankful for your group of friends, as they reflect who you are. Certain friends arrive at different times of your life, according to how you feel. If you are "down and out" you might attract "down and out" friends. Showing positivity will attract positive friends. Be an unconditional friend without expecting anything in return. Invest in your friendships. Provide advice and assistance whenever necessary. It's a great blessing to advise and support others. Don't try to buy friendship, as that is a sign of personal insecurity. Appreciate the friends you have and always be approachable. No matter what, show a good face to all. Most of all, avoid toxic friends, those who pose a negative influence. Gossipers, pessimists, and jealous people can bring you down. If a friend has those tendencies, it may affect you in a negative way. Try to help, but from a distance. Most of all, thank Hashem for your good "Friends", as a good friend is better than precious oil.

Love, Daddy

PEARLS OF WISDOM

"The proper way to acquire wisdom is to channel our minds to keep the commandments of the Torah."

My Dear Children,

Another great gift from Hashem is a clear mind. Your brain is billions of times greater than any computer. Every item that is deposited in your brain leaves an everlasting impression for your future. If you only visit healthy websites, your computer will have a clear hard drive. However, if you visit injurious websites, your computer will eventually crash due to a virus. The same is true for your precious human mind. That's a good reason to stay away from toxic people and anyone (or any group) who will negatively affect your life or confuse your thinking. At times, these people may seem exciting, but that is an illusion. Surround yourself with good people. Trust your instincts; be good; be someone who others can count on, and be patient. Have discipline, good manners, and the ethics you were brought up with.[39] Always greet people nicely. Try to learn something new every day. Reading, writing, and praying will maintain a healthy hard drive, clear of viruses. Always appreciate all you are blessed with, express gratitude to Hashem and please don't take Him for granted. A clear, concise mind will be the result of the precious "Pearls of Wisdom" from Hashem.

Love, Daddy

THE POWER OF FORGIVENESS

"A humble person overcomes his pride and forgives others."

My Dear Children,

When people do something that hurts you, it's easy to get angry and hold a grudge. However, everything that happens in life, good or bad, is Hashem's way of educating you. Getting annoyed or angry is a normal reaction, but holding a grudge won't serve any purpose. If you can find it in your heart to forgive them, do it sincerely. It will make your life easier, because holding a grudge takes away your focus from the good things in life. Forgiving others will help you move on. Don't get me wrong, you don't have to be best friends with them. but if you can forgive them for hurting you, you can also forgive yourself for things that you regret. Never hurt someone on purpose. If you hurt someone unintentionally, always apologize. Just as you should not hold a grudge against others, you should not feel guilty about things you've done. Once you've taken responsibility and apologized, let it go. Guilt can be a positive trait, as it enforces repentance, but it can also be negative, if you hold onto it too long. When you go to sleep at night, please say the prayer of declaration to forgive others.[40] Imitate Hashem as He will always forgive you. That's the "Power of Forgiveness."

Love, Daddy

STARTING OVER

"Repentance causes Hashem to respond with forgiveness."

My Dear Children,

One of the greatest gifts Hashem has given you is the opportunity to repent for sins and start over. At night, you go to sleep tired, and awake eager and ready to approach a new day. The gift of repentance is miraculous. You can sin, and all you must do is admit what you've done and try not to do it again. After repentance, you are like a newborn baby.[41] When you start over, try to let go of past pain, both pains caused by you and caused by others. Be thankful for the chance to start fresh and let go of grudges and guilt. Forgive yourself and forgive others, just as Hashem forgives you. Appreciate all the wonderful things in your life. You are lovely and loving people, but you're not perfect. Should you fall, get back up. If this is difficult, please reach out to someone who can help you. And, of course, pray to Hashem to give you strength and thank Him for the opportunity of "Starting Over."

Love, Daddy

HOPE AND DETERMINATION

"Prayer is the most effective vehicle to reverse adversity."

My Dear Children,

What happens when one has a life changing experience? What happens when a person is sent a test that he feels he can't handle? What happens when a person feels so distant, that he loses hope... and how can you help bring that hope back? First, remind him that there are still good things in life and suggest that he hold onto the thought of even just one as a survival tool. For example, remind him that he has beautiful children, loving parents, or friends that want to help. Remind him of all the good in the world. And, of course, remind him that Hashem is always there, and to have faith and pray that things will improve.[42] Try to help him concentrate on one precious thing in his life and give him the determination to create change. Remind him that this is just a test from Hashem that will lead to growth, and that Hashem would not give him a test that he could not handle. Finally, remind him that praying is a connection to Hashem to increase "Hope and Determination".

Love, Daddy

HEALERS

"Proper social environments maintain spiritual health."

My Dear Children,

It is inevitable that at some point we all experience loss. It can be very distressing, but Hashem has taught us the stages of mourning. It's about faith and trying to draw closer to Hashem during this terribly difficult process. Healing takes time and requires faith.[43] Please don't try to fight the healing process, by self-medicating or developing unhealthy habits. Don't try to jump ahead in the healing process. You can't get better overnight. Just stay strong and reach out for guidance. Speak to a Rabbi, friend, sibling or anyone who has your best interests at heart. If someone who is grieving comes to you for help, do whatever you can to make the grieving process easier. Remind him that Hashem is the ultimate "Healer," and He's always there to help.

Love, Daddy

TEAMWORK

"Successful organizations are results of hard work and teamwork."

My Dear Children,

You are blessed to live in the most generous community on this planet. If someone is in a challenging situation, whether it's physical, emotional, financial, or spiritual, assistance is just a phone call away. The value of teamwork is the foundation of our community. Most other communities don't support each other like we do. Each person looks after himself and his family, and they don't even know their neighbors. We take care of our entire community, because we have faith in each other. Hashem wants to see us growing as a group.[44] The value of a minyan is to demonstrate dependency on others. It is up to you and your generation to keep our community as it has always been. Always lend a helping hand to others. Support those in need. Give advice and always be honest when conducting business. Judge others favorably, just be aware of people who want to divide your team. Luckily in our community, this doesn't happen often. So, thank Hashem for being born into a community dedicated to "Teamwork," where members understand the value of taking care of each other, and being part of a team.

Love, Daddy

RAINDROPS FROM HEAVEN

"Rain is responsible for the food we eat, the clothes we wear, and the houses we build."

My Dear Children,

At some time in your life, it's likely that financial issues will arise. Please remember that everything you have comes from Hashem.[45] He is responsible for the wealth you receive and the job that you have. He blesses each person with talents that should be used to pursue a career. If you are not making enough money, maybe you need to find another opportunity. Look for hidden messages from Hashem and act on them. Know that He will not let you starve. And don't let financial insecurity lead you to illegal activities. Please have faith in Hashem, be patient, and never take an illegal route to wealth. Your word and integrity are most important in Hashem's eyes. You must understand that financial well-being will arrive at the right time, when Hashem deems it so. In the meantime, have faith and express gratitude towards Hashem. In response, Hashem will always send you "Raindrops from Heaven."

Love, Daddy

AND JUSTICE FOR ALL

"Officers and law enforcement prevent anarchy in the streets."

My Dear Children,

One of the foundations of Judaism is our legacy. The Torah gave us our traditions. We stand when we see our Rabbis. We respect the elderly. When we were young, we learned not to talk back to our elders. It taught us humility. Rabbis and elderly people represent our Torah, religion, and tradition. We were taught that respect doesn't mean that you always have to agree with others. It's okay to disagree as long as it's done respectfully. Reverence for our Rabbis and elders has kept our community together. In addition, please respect the law and its officers. When you approach a police officer, thank him! Even if he gives you a ticket. Without them, there would be chaos. We need officers and law enforcement bodies to protect society.[46] Unfortunately, we are living in a time of corruption. Things may seem unfair, but have confidence that even though it may seem unfair, Hashem is the true judge; and, if you act humbly, you will be rewarded. Hashem will provide, as He is all about truth "And Justice for All".

Love, Daddy

The Elementary School I attended as a boy.

CONNECTIONS TO THE PAST

"Respect for elders are essential foundations set up by our ancestors."

My Dear Children,

Our community arrived here 100 years ago. Our Rabbis could have been lenient and let everyone assimilate as they saw fit; however, they knew that they had to make strict rules for our heritage to continue. Had they not done so, there might not be a community today. We were taught to love Hashem and follow the Torah. If you ever become too distracted to attend Synagogue or follow the Torah, please remember your connection to your parents, grandparents, and their descendants. They set up a system for us, so that we could live better lives with faith and peace of mind. And they made sure that our Rabbis are not only extremely learned, but always willing to help everyone in the community, in any way possible.[47] If you're extremely lucky, you will find a Rabbi whom you trust, respect, and revere – a Rabbi you can develop a personal relationship with. We all need someone who can help us objectively with our daily challenges. Some Rabbis may not blend with your personality, and that's fine. Just keep looking until you find the one who you think would make an excellent mentor – a Rabbi who knows when to be extra strict with you and when to be lenient. And when someone comes to you asking for advice, try emulating those traits. As you excel in leadership, always remain humble, and never forget to thank Hashem for the foundation set up by our ancestors. By doing so, you will maintain "Connections to the Past."

Love, Daddy

BEHIND THE SCENES

*"Technological advances can interrupt one's belief that Hashem
is running everything."*

My Dear Children,

Thanks to our wonderful community and ancestry, from the time
you were born, you were steeped in a foundation of religion and
beautiful traditions, but there may be a time when your faith in
Hashem will be tested. The most effective way to pass a test is
a constant investment in Torah education and spirituality. You
will know people with different religious beliefs. If they try to
lure you towards their way of thinking, don't debate them.[48] They
are entitled to their religious beliefs, as you are entitled to yours.
However, don't allow them to make you question your beliefs.
This will harm your spiritual growth. Should this happen, please
speak with a Rabbi. Once you are in a better place you will start to
notice hidden and obvious miracles happening directly to you. Stay
confident in yourself and the beliefs we instilled in you. You will
always have faith, once you realize that Hashem is orchestrating
everything "Behind the Scenes."

Love, Daddy

HOME SWEET HOME

"Spending quality time at home establishes permanent roots within our souls."

My Dear Children,

Your greatest assets in your life will be your spouse, children, and your home life. A house is a home when every family member is grateful that they're together around the dinner table.[49] Appreciate the moments you might take for granted in this fast-paced world. Appreciate your spouse sitting with you; enjoy your children running around in their pajamas. Savor the quality time you spend helping your kids with their homework, and then putting them to sleep. These are the times that matter most. Mutual respect between you and your spouse will create a foundation that can transform a house into a home. Our ancestors spent their lives fleeing from one country to another due to hatred and persecution. We are fortunate enough to live in a country free of persecution, where we can be practicing Jews, and where we can earn a living. Our lives are so simple compared to the lives of our ancestors, yet they were thankful to Hashem for all that they had. We should be extra grateful for all the peaceful and sacred moments in our lives. Please be sure to express gratitude daily to Hashem for providing you with a country where you are free to live in a home with your beautiful family, and have a mezuzah on your doorpost without fear of persecution. We are so lucky to have a "Home Sweet Home" where we can invite the Divine Presence inside.

Love, Daddy

SEEDS OF SUCCESS

"A seed doesn't turn into a sunflower overnight."

My Dear Children,

Think of your life as a bank account, and each day contemplate how you spent your energy (spiritual money), because you are investing in your future every day. Mitzvahs give you positive credits. Learning a page of Torah every day can build up your balance in a hurry. However, spending money and time irresponsibly, eating unhealthy foods, and not doing your best at work will take away a few credits. Being disrespectful to others and giving in to addictions, such as smoking, drinking, and doing drugs can wipe out your entire balance. If you try your best to always keep your balance in the positive, yet you still do not see the fruits of your "investments", please be patient and have faith in Hashem it will come. Until then, be proud of yourself for being a good person. That is an accomplishment.

Mom and I began investing in your future the day you were born. You live in a great community where you received an excellent education. You should always have a plan, even if it is small, and at the right time, the seeds will flourish. The seeds you plant will have everlasting results.[50] You have been educated and live in a great community. Learn from your parents, Rabbis, and ancestors that small investments are "Seeds of Success" for you and future generations.

Love, Daddy

HEALTH IS WEALTH

"True wealth is one of exceptional physical and emotional health."

My Dear Children,

It's easy to take your health for granted when you're healthy. In life, we should never take anything for granted – especially our health – because that can change in an instant.[51] If you were born with 10 fingers, 10 toes, and every other part of your body in the right place, that was Hashem's gift to you. Therefore, each morning when we wake, we should thank Hashem for everything He's given us, especially our health – both physical and mental! If you encounter a mental or physical challenge, please continue to pray, and make sure others will pray for you. Hashem has the power to heal you. A clear mind can be close to Hashem. "Health is Wealth" is the best attitude to have.

Love, Daddy

ELECTRIC DREAMS

"Prayers serve as the best vehicle to invite the glory of Hashem into our homes."

My Dear Children,

A peaceful and loving home life is an exceptional goal to strive for. After that, everything is secondary. As you grow up, you and your siblings will move on. You will have your own spouse and children. As your responsibilities increase, please don't forget the foundation set up by earlier generations. Stay close to your siblings and all of your relatives. Help and protect each other when necessary. Be a close-knit family. Celebrate birthdays and anniversaries together. These are moments you will cherish for the rest of your lives.[52] Please never allow outsiders to tear you apart. Even if your sibling is wrong, please be the better person and pursue peace. Never be jealous of each other. The greatest prayer of a parent is to ensure his children will remain close. There is nothing more upsetting than to see your children at odds with each other. Try not to have petty arguments, and if you do, please don't let them linger or hold a grudge. Say what you must, then hug and make up. If an argument starts, please pray to Hashem to give you humility to diffuse it. The key to staying close is a humble spirit. Prayer is the best vehicle. Prayer is not visible, but it's "Electric Dreams" that pierce the heavens.

Love, Daddy

PART 4

THE FOURTH HIGHWAY
OF THE SOUL:
STAYING THE COURSE

October 2007- October 2008

A t this point in my life, I was trying to decide whether I would make the choice to stay the course or get off at the next exit. The next exit meant move to California and start a new life. During this time, my Rabbis and friends always made sure I had a place to be on Shabbat and Holidays. When my kids were with me, my mom would prepare meals for us and send it to Brooklyn. Sometimes she would drive it in herself just to go back to Deal, New Jersey. Other times, we would go to Deal and have Shabbat and Holidays together. I was never alone. I would observe Shabbat and go out to NYC immediately after sundown. The religion, community, friends, and my career kept me on the correct road, but deep down, I wanted a different life. Luckily, Hashem started to take over by causing me to see His hand. Every time I went out with my friends in NYC, I would find a ticket on my car, or my car would be towed or broken into, etc. It was a clear sign that Hashem didn't want to let me go. "Staying the Course" was my only option.

I hope you find these next set of letters useful for when you are at a crossroads or need encouragement to keep on course.

LIFE'S DESTINATIONS

"Sometimes the long, uncomfortable journey is better than a shortcut."

My Dear Children,

As you become adults, it's good to think about where you want to be in 10 or 15 years. You can even make plans to get you there. What you must realize is that Hashem can change those plans in the blink of an eye. When you're forced into such a scenario, for whatever reason, you may feel confused and uncertain. Things may seem chaotic and out of control. My best advice is to adapt and plan an alternate course. Then maintain your focus on your new destination. Have faith that Hashem is preparing your journey. He may have different ideas but have faith it's for your own good. He could be testing you or helping you appreciate the journey. This creates humility, because it forces you to realize that you are not in charge, and you never were. It's okay to try and change your journey, but if there is too much resistance, perhaps Hashem may be telling you that you're headed on the wrong course.[53] Maybe you'll still get where you wanted to go, but by taking a different route. Your goal in life should be to live in the service of Hashem and His commandments. "Life's Destinations" may have detours and forks, but it's all a journey home.

Love, Daddy

PEACE OF MIND

"Faith and prayer will achieve world peace and true peace of mind."

My Dear Children,

The most important thing in life, other than your family, is your peace of mind. Without it, life will be chaos. Technology has its benefits, but it can add to the chaos. You can become a slave to your phone, email, and social media, so use it sparingly and wisely. The Internet damages relationships and wastes huge amounts of time. When you arrive home after a long day at the office, put your phone away. Never bring it to the table, as dinnertime should be used to share a delicious meal and reconnect with your loved ones. Technology should just be a tool to benefit your business and society. The greatest gift we have is Shabbat. It is a day when we shut out the rest of the world to concentrate on family. It is a time of reflection. As you age and reflect on your life, you will remember happy times shared with family and friends, not the amount of time you spent on social media. Technology is a great advancement, but don't let it take away your "Peace of Mind."[54]

Love, Daddy

EXPRESSIONS

"In order to receive kindness from heaven, one must conquer the negative expressions of his heart."

My Dear Children,

Texts and emails make it easier to act bolder and say things we would not say in person or on the phone. If a text conversation gets negative, my advice is to stop it before you say something you will regret. People are sensitive, so it's important to be polite. Remove exclamations, capital letters and emotional icons that could hurt someone's feelings. It is hard to take words back when you've sent them via email. The way you express yourself is the way others perceive you. Hashem gave you the power of words; use them carefully and wisely.[55] We are taught never to embarrass another person, yet, on the Internet, especially when people can be anonymous, it's easy to write mean things. Resist! Please don't send that text or email. Request the strength to be a very good person. Express gratitude and humility. It's fine to use emails and texts to communicate, but just remember to be polite and not to let another goad you into a battle of words. Everything lives forever on the Internet. Don't write something you don't want others to read! Only use positive "Expressions" and Hashem will reciprocate positively!

Love, Daddy

FOOD FOR THOUGHT

"We are Hashem's guests in this world; everything is miraculously prepared with love for us."

My Dear Children,

One of the foundations of our community, and one of life's greatest privileges, is a home filled with family and friends on Shabbat and holidays.[56] We all want to do everything we can for our family and friends, and for our community as well. If you ever notice someone having a hard time, invite him to join your family for Shabbat. You will bring him hope and strength. Your home will be blessed, and your family too. Your children will witness your mitzvah and imitate you. They will learn from your actions. Our community was built on an "all for one" attitude. If you are not able to welcome someone, for whatever reason, send him food for Shabbat, or make sure his refrigerator is full. It will preserve his dignity. "Food for Thought": please reciprocate and help others emulate Hashem.

Love, Daddy

THE NEXT GENERATION

"To ensure our legacy, we are obligated to teach Torah to our children."

My Dear Children,

Always remember your legacy was started by our ancestors who built this community and made sure we take our heritage very seriously. Please imitate them. It's one of the most important fundamentals of Judaism. It's written in the Shema. Strive to observe the Holy Torah, connect with and continue to honor Rabbis, give charity to institutions, and maintain a reflection of our parents and grandparents. When you have children, please teach them about religion and our heritage, so that they can continue our beautiful traditions then hand them on to their children and grandchildren.[57] One thing that really matters is watching "The Next Generation" perpetuate our G-d given legacy.

Love, Daddy

Our iconic synagogue in Bradley Beach.

RELIGIOUS ROOTS

"Pure character traits can establish roots within us and our children."

My Dear Children,

Please always make sure to live in a neighborhood that believes in religion, and has synagogues, schools, friends, and community. These things are the greatest protection against assimilation. You may receive a job offer that will require extreme traveling, sometimes causing you to be away from family and community for long ranges of time. Please bear in mind, that although money is important, being away, and sacrificing religion, can be detrimental to you and to your family's spiritual survival.[58] Children imitate parents and as they see you steering away from religion, they will do the same. No job opportunity is worth assimilation. One small sacrifice can grow, and before you know it, you might be financially wealthy, but spiritually poor. Our ancestors gave up so much for us. When they arrived in America, some had to sacrifice parts of their religion to support their families, and had to forego Torah study and much more just to survive. We can understand the reason, but now there are many institutions that exist to make sure that you don't have to do that. Perpetuating "Religious Roots" reinforces your contract with Hashem at Sinai. Try to remember that wealth is nice but doesn't compare to our religious heritage.

Love, Daddy

LOST AND FOUND

"Our ancestors went against the grain; through loss they found Hashem and his Torah."

My Dear Children,

If you experience loss, I hope you can return to your routine very soon. It can be a job loss, a sports injury, or a life changing situation. Honestly, the only effective tool when experiencing loss is faith and surrendering to Hashem. He knows what is best for you and has a larger plan.[59] Dealing with loss is part of the growth process. Without faith it can be a winding road to nowhere. Extreme loss without faith in Hashem can lead to self-medication just to get through the day. This may seem to help; however, acting in this manner is not part of the growth process. It is quite the opposite. You need outlets, but healthy ones. Allow friends to help you get though the difficult days, and don't lose faith in Hashem. Instead, open your heart to Him. Loss is a reminder of man's vulnerability. Our forefathers suffered through loss, but even in the darkest times, they turned to G-d for strength. Faith is an effective way to help locate the "Lost and Found" areas in your life. With that in mind, everything lost will be found.

Love, Daddy

FREE ADMISSION

"Thanking Hashem helps us realize that He is running the world to the smallest detail."

My Dear Children,

One of the most draining experiences in life is feeling indebted to people. You must constantly thank them and seek their approval, which can cause tremendous insecurity. Please pray daily that you won't feel like you depend on anyone or anything for your livelihood, other than Hashem. Hashem created you with special talents that you should utilize for your success. It's up to you to discover them.[60] If people help you, they certainly deserve gratitude and appreciation. But nobody owns you! It's best to be independent and work hard, so that you can always be proud of who you are. That doesn't mean that you should never ask for help. There are so many wonderful organizations in our community that exist to help us. If you're honest, work hard, and you're accountable for all your actions, you will earn the respect of everyone around you, and when you need help, people will be happy to assist you. Alternately, when you help others, you can earn a "Free Admission" ticket towards a legacy of greatness.

Love, Daddy

FACE TO FACE

"The beauty of the universe brings us face to face with the greatness of our Creator."

My Dear Children,

As you pay attention to your daily activities, you will see the hand of Hashem. He cares about you and is involved in every decision you make and everything that happens to you. All you must do is pray! As things seem more challenging, pray more! Hashem loves to hear your prayers, and more than anything, he loves the humility that goes into them. Praying is clear testimony that you believe that only He can save you. Sometimes you may feel disappointed that your prayers are not being answered. This may be because the timing is off or that Hashem has other plans. We can never understand His full picture.

Try not to get angry, jealous, or stubborn when things don't get better as fast as you would like. These traits will only hold you back. Instead, invest your time in learning and appreciating all that G-d has blessed you with. If you are having a tough day, learning Torah can make you feel better, changing negative feelings to positive ones. Be compassionate to others and spread peace. Pray with a minyan and form bonds of friendship and teamwork. If you see someone in a bad place, try to assist him. We are all responsible for each other! It is always important to demonstrate kindness, even when we're feeling challenged. These valuable traits make Hashem very happy. If you look closely enough, you will see miracles all around you, which will bring you "Face to Face" with Hashem's benevolence and create an everlasting bond.[61]

Love, Daddy

BASIC ELEMENTS

"Noticing the harmony in nature helps us see the kindness and compassion of the Almighty."

My Dear Children,

The most important components of Judaism are unity and peace. Always maintain and spread peace among family, friends, and community members.[62] It pleases Hashem tremendously to see his children working together in harmony. Try to avoid conflict with others. Sometimes it is difficult, but the key to preventing confrontation is humility. Try to avoid anger. It is like a fire that destroys everything it touches. Pride and jealousy also cause many arguments. Jealousy is a lack of faith in Hashem and in yourself. When you feel jealous, look inside yourself to find out what's behind this feeling. You have so much love and infinite blessings in your life. What could you possibly be jealous of? Try to replace this very negative trait with faith in Hashem. Faith is the realization that Hashem is behind every situation. Imitating the traits of love for one another is a "Basic Element" trait that puts out the fire of anger and pride.

Love, Daddy

BIRDS OF A FEATHER

"Proper atmosphere and associations are vital to one's character development and growth."

My Dear Children,

We have been blessed with a great community and a great religion. We have been fortunate enough to be together as a family. If people in the community are having difficulty, we have the best organizations to assist them. We are one as a nation, community, and family. Please express your constant gratitude to Hashem for this gift. We are all for one and one for all. If you are ever challenged, always remember that we must be different from the outside world. The commandments of the Torah are a guide to life. If at any time you get frustrated by the community and want to move away, please don't! Nothing is perfect. Please weigh the positives and negatives. We live by certain rules to protect us from society. Our commandments should be studied and learned daily. You are a servant of Hashem. Please remain a loyal servant. If you see others in trouble, try to help them.[63] If you can't assist them, at least guide them to a Rabbi who can. If there is trouble in our community or nation, please try your best to help. A community that flocks like "Birds of a Feather" demonstrates loyalty to Hashem. This makes Hashem very happy, and you will be rewarded tremendously.

Love, Daddy

שובה אלי בי גאלתיך

During my darkest time, I saw the writing on the wall of a Synagogue in NYC. Translated it means: Return to me, for I have redeemed you.

PART 5

THE FIFTH HIGHWAY
OF THE SOUL:
FOLLOWING THE SIGNS

October 2008 - October 2009

During this time, I started to see open miracles. The reason I started to see these signs was due to my eyes opening and accepting that straying from my faith would be an uphill battle towards a life of emptiness. Still, the gravitational pull to the other side was continuing to cause me to make U–Turns on the highway. The road became slippery, and I knew I was headed for an accident. I met a Rabbi and told him what I was going through. He told me that Hashem was not letting me go. He advised me to meet with him every Shabbat at 1 p.m. to discuss my journey. I decided it was time for a full court press towards religion. From there, wherever the car led me, is where I would go. I started listening to CDs, going to classes, and learning more intensely. My prayers were much stronger as I pleaded with Hashem to put me on the right path. I started to get very close to the Rabbis of our community. I was learning that "Following the Signs" of the Torah and its commandments was the only way to go.

May the following letters inspire you to recognize and follow the signs Hashem is sending you.

AGAINST THE GRAIN

"During challenging times, one must go against the grain and push backwards to move forward."

My Dear Children,

We all act on impulse. Children just react, because they are not able to differentiate one situation from another. As we age, we learn right from wrong. The ability to control our instincts and emotions is what differentiates us from all other animals. At times, wrong may seem much more alluring than right, and that's when control is needed. There will be times in your life when you will have to control your emotions, control your tongue, and hold back feelings that you would much rather act upon. It's a difficult task, but most rewarding. For example, you may receive a call at night to assist someone, and you might feel too tired to go out and help him. It's easy to say, "We will deal with it tomorrow." However, a true leader says, "I will be right there." Someone may insult you, and you might want to insult him right back, but if you're able to hold your tongue and remain silent, chances are you'll be happy you did.

Often these situations are tests from Hashem to bring you to a higher level. You possess an unbelievable amount of strength; however, if a test is too difficult, please pray to Hashem to assist you. Once you control your nature, Hashem will change nature for you, and you will see miracles.[64] It's not always easy to go "Against the Grain" of your nature, but Hashem is there to help.

Love, Daddy

MUSICAL PRAYER

"The power of prayer rings a bell in heaven."

My Dear Children,

The best answer to most of your challenges is to unlock the key to Hashem's heart through prayer. Tehilim (aka Psalms) has the power to shake the heavens. Singing praise to Hashem arouses His mercy and causes Him to judge favorably. Tehilim can change a person from sickness to recovery in seconds. Tehilim starts with a foundation of faith. It teaches you to avoid evil people, bad advice, and bad surroundings. That is the first step in connecting to Hashem.[65] You need that foundation to grow spiritually. You are praised for avoiding the worldly temptations that remove you from true spirituality. If you are experiencing a challenge in your life that seems overwhelming, please reach out to a Rabbi to assist you. When you are praying and feel that you are not being answered, please have faith that Hashem knows when to answer. Keep praying. Tehilim is the best "Musical Prayer" to Hashem.

Love, Daddy

PURE ELEMENT

"A healthy atmosphere will maintain healthy brain function, free of toxic material."

My Dear Children,

Today everything is becoming organic – food, clothing, cosmetics, etc. People want to be healthier. That's completely understandable. In order to be truly healthy, in addition to eating organic foods and exercising, one needs self-confidence, prayer, and to do good deeds. You should also strive to keep your mind organic – clean from detrimental beliefs and environments. Life is complex and there may come a time when you feel disconnected from Hashem and spirituality. Money and material items may tempt you. Spending money on family and friends may make you feel good, but just remember without some sort of spirituality, eventually you're going to feel very empty. If you are faced with such a challenge, keep praying and turn to those who love you most. Try to have faith in Hashem. You are a pure organic soul. Keep it that way, and always thank Hashem for everything He gives you. Try not to take anything for granted. Technology can be great, and it can be distracting. Please use it wisely and organically. Be aware of everything you feed into your brain. Whatever you feed into your brain is how it will react. Keep your mind clean and with "Pure Elements" of faith, and then you will be able to serve Hashem with a clear mind.[66]

Love, Daddy

LADDERS TO HASHEM

"Man's behavior on earth has a spiritual reflection in heaven."

My Dear Children,

As you grow spiritually, unfortunately, your evil inclination will grow as well; and if you're not careful, it can engulf you. Spiritually, you will want to connect to G-d, while your evil inclination will want to connect to materialism. The body and soul may be in constant battle for your entire life. My best advice is to make sure you pray every day, and set aside time to learn and demonstrate kindness to others. Being kind to others is very important, because it's a way to show Hashem that you are imitating His ways. If, instead, you give in to materialism, it can lead you down a dark road to wanting more pleasure than spirituality. This often leads to, G-d forbid, addiction. Smoking, drugs, gambling, drinking, or any other vice can bring you away from spirituality, away from Hashem, and away from heaven. If you ever feel connected to materialism, stop and think about what you're doing. Think about your blessings and how good Hashem is. Then learn more, demonstrate kindness, and have faith.[67] Acknowledge that only Hashem provides for our needs. He is the one to depend on. It's not easy, but it is necessary. Talk to Hashem, write down your feelings, and never be ashamed to ask for help. All these tools are ladders towards heaven to connect you to Hashem. You will win some and lose some, but keep moving up the "Ladder to Hashem"!

Love, Daddy

MIRROR REFLECTIONS

"True blessing occurs when two opposites work harmoniously towards a common goal."

My Dear Children,

During your lifetime you will meet many people, and the one that you are closest to will become a mirror reflection of yourself. You will notice as you get close to someone, people will say that you look alike. Since you are so close, you are imitating their actions subconsciously. During this journey, you may meet the wrong person. It could be a friend, a business associate, or someone you are interested in romantically. If you start to mimic each other's actions, it could hurt you physically and spiritually. Physically you will feel drained, since you are not living up to your potential. Spiritually, it can dampen your connection to Hashem. My humble advice is to associate with people who bring out the best in you. If, unfortunately, you are in a challenging situation, don't give up.[68] Reach out to others and pray profusely to save you from the evil inclination. At the same time, try to find a better environment. With prayer and a better social group, hopefully you will get back on track. "Mirror Reflections" of Hashem is imitating His ways of kindness and clinging to spirituality.

Love, Daddy

EXPRESSIONS OF GRATITUDE

"Proper emotional, physical, and spiritual health are necessary components of survival."

My Dear Children,

Please, always thank Hashem for everything. The Gomel blessing applies to rescue from imprisonment, traveling through a desert, traveling over an ocean, or recovering from a sickness. It corresponds to the four elements of the earth: Fire, Air, Water and Dust.[69]

If you ever feel like you've lost your spirituality, please beg Hashem for help. Please connect to a Rabbi, mentor, or friends who will assist you. Thanking Hashem in advance is also essential. An ounce of prevention is worth a pound of cure. Too many people have been lost because they couldn't or wouldn't ask for support. You are part of a great community and there are organizations that want to help you. All you must do is ask. Appreciating the gifts Hashem has bestowed upon you will create a close connection of faith. Staying away from negativity, keeping calm, increasing your learning, and realizing you are never alone are "Expressions of Gratitude" because you will realize Hashem is there.

Love, Daddy

SPIRITUAL WINDMILLS

"Creating kindness and hospitality for the less fortunate strengthens the links of a chain."

My Dear Children,

At some point in your life, there may be an old friend or a contemporary in need of assistance. Whether he's going through a life-changing event or he is just feeling lonely, please try to help him. Don't abandon him because you're too busy, help him. Our community possesses the finest support systems. We are a kind and caring community, built on helping each other. Losing just one person to drugs or intermarriage is like losing a link in a chain.

The community is connected in many ways. We were all taught as children to help those around us, so that they can get better and help others. As a community we believe in prayer, spirituality, learning and teaching proper ethics and faith. Please don't let anyone be pulled away from Hashem. Like a strong chain, we are all linked. We are like spiritual windmills, moving others towards Hashem. Keep the wind blowing in a healthy direction.[70] When we act as "Spiritual Windmills," we are emulating our ancestors and our Creator.

Love, Daddy

SPARKS

"Opening doors for others will ignite a spark in heaven."

My Dear Children,

When you were young, you were taught the importance of religion. As you grew older and your religious education continued, you kept feeling closer and closer to Hashem. However, when you grow into adulthood, circumstances will change. You will get jobs, have families, and sometimes during everyday life, religion may take a backseat to these things. It doesn't happen all at once. It's a degeneration process that can take years. Just remember, should this happen, Hashem will never abandon you. You have sparks of Hashem that will never go out. If you know someone who is falling, please reassure him that Hashem will never let him go. It's important to reassure him that you, too, will be there for him. Inspire him to maintain hope and advise him to connect with a Rabbi. Please don't judge him; just do your best to keep him close. Every Jew has a spark inside that never goes out. Advise him and pray for him to find his way back to Hashem with your sparks of holiness.[71] Please help others with their challenges and their "Sparks" will be reignited.

Love, Daddy

One of our main synagogues in Deal, NJ

THE LEGACY CONTINUES

"Educational institutions are the driving forces to perpetuate our legacy."

My Dear Children,

It's a very good idea to learn the history of our community and our nation. We survived many persecutions. Our ancestors gave their lives for our religion. Despite the challenges, our nation is still here and doing better. G-d made a promise to us that although we make mistakes, He will never abandon us. It's easy to remember this when things are going well. It's more difficult when we're going through challenges. When faced with any sort of obstacle, take it as an opportunity for growth.

You are born with exceptional traits. Use them to better yourself, our community, and our nation. Your mission in life is quite easy – educate your children and encourage them to be proud of who they are. Establish a routine that allows you to spend quality time with your family. Teach your children about their ancestry. Make them happy to get close to Hashem. Please instill faith and confidence in them. Our children are our future. Sacrifice whatever is necessary to give them the love that they need and deserve. Teach them that when "The Legacy Continues," they perpetuate the nation, serve Hashem, and bring kindness to the world.[72]

Love, Daddy

PART 6

THE SIXTH HIGHWAY OF THE SOUL: CROSSING THE BRIDGE

October 2009- February 2011

As I paid the tolls and crossed the bridge, I started to appreciate our grandparents and leaders of our community. I started to better appreciate the edict established by Rabbi Jacob S. Kassin^{ZT"L} as a community that works symbiotically. We are One Man/One Heart. Now that I was on the other side of the bridge, life changed. My son David got married. I traveled to Israel for the first time. It was a spiritual journey back home into Hashem's arms. After my trip, on June 11, 2010, unfortunately my dad passed away. I followed my dad's advice to always move on and ahead. I decided to change my life by finding an apartment; it became the beginning of my personal redemption. Once I

"Crossed the Bridge", I couldn't turn back. I am where I am now, in a much better place spiritually, financially, and physically.

The letters that follow describe how to live day-to-day with honor and grace.

TREASURE CHEST IN HEAVEN

"The Torah and its teachings are an eternal reward for future generations."

My Dear Children.

Life in our community has become easy. It was not so for the older generation. 100 years ago, our ancestors faced many challenges, including poverty. Community members had to live out of town to earn a living. The tragedy was the threat of assimilation. Parents had to watch their children go to war. It was a life of sacrifice. The reason we are standing today is because they had faith in Hashem. If you, G-d forbid, ever consider turning away from religion, please ask yourself, How can a person do that to their grandparent's legacy? Our lifestyle is an investment into the future. Money can come and go, but our legacy is forever. One person who goes astray is equal to losing generations. If you see someone who has turned away from religion, try to help him. Don't judge him! Maybe he just wants to be heard. The investment of our grandparents is your "Treasure Chest in Heaven." Now, it's up to you to keep it full.[73]

Love, Daddy

TAKE TIME TO
SLOW DOWN AND RELAX

"A day of rest teaches us that Hashem is the source of all our sustenance."

My Dear Children,

One of Hashem's greatest gifts is Shabbat.[74] Technology has overtaken our lives, so much so that it is often impossible to sit down and relax. Thank G-d when Shabbat arrives and the cell phones are turned off. Computers are shut down and it's a marvelous opportunity for reflection. There are few things in life as lovely as Shabbat dinner with the family and without distractions. It's a time to sit with the family and spend quality time with each other. It's the perfect time to talk with your children. Discuss topics that will help them grow up with confidence, religion, and exceptional character traits. It's important to realize just how important the Shabbat table is. It is the center stage, a place to gear up for the following week and reflect on the past week. Inviting family and friends is a great way to connect with them, as well. Appreciate the time you have been given to "Sit Down and Relax" and express gratitude to Hashem for the blessing of Shabbat.

Love, Daddy

THE IMPORTANCE OF GRATITUDE

"An accomplished student is a teacher's reward."

My Dear Children,

Nothing happens by accident. It is all Hashem's doing. As a child you were fed, dressed, and taken care of. After you grew up, your responsibilities increased, and you became the provider. Responsibility creates humility. It is very important to learn the importance of gratitude toward others. We often tend to take those closest to us – our spouses, families, employees and even our friends – for granted. If you have employees, always thank them. Thanking others creates bonds of friendship and loyalty. It creates humility and teaches you not to take people for granted. Please thank Hashem for everything He gives you. Think about all the miracles Hashem performs for you on a minute-to-minute basis. Look at your eyes, ears, nose, mouth, your ability to walk, talk, etc. All these abilities are gifts from Hashem.

Thanking others prevents arrogance. Hashem doesn't like arrogant people. Train your children to say thank you. Thank a waiter in a restaurant or a policeman, even if he gives you a ticket. He is trying to teach you to be safe. Please don't be an ingrate. Once you thank others, you will be thanked for your kindness as well. Gratitude brings you closer to Hashem and is a most valuable character trait. Most of all thank Hashem daily for your sustenance.[75] Thank Him for the small things, and He will continue to send blessings. "The Importance of Gratitude" will bring about a happier life.

Love, Daddy

THE HUMBLE WAVE

"Accepting divine decree with humility is like diving under a wave."

My Dear Children,

There may be times in your life when you will be in a comfortable situation but confused whether it's best for you to remain comfortable or move on. There will be pros and cons for each choice. Please pay attention to the signs. If you suddenly feel resistance, or like something needs to change, chances are Hashem is sending you a hidden message. At this point, you must remember to surrender yourself with humility before Hashem.[76] When approaching an oncoming wave, bow into the wave instead of trying to fight it. The key is humility. You should pray to Hashem to show you the right direction. It is important to realize that just like a father, Hashem loves you. Hashem wants you safe. The feelings of resistance may feel frustrating, but it is Hashem telling you that He wants something better for you. All you must do is take a leap of faith and stop fighting fate, because it's a losing proposition. Unfortunately, there are times that a person will use his free will and decide not to listen to Hashem's messages. If that happens, Hashem may stop sending them, as He doesn't involve himself with man's free will. My best advice is when you see a wave crashing toward you, bow your head in prayer, faith, and humility and create "The Humble Wave."

Love, Daddy

LET'S MAKE A DEAL

"Bowing our heads in humility and acceptance is true faith."

My Dear Children,

If you are going through a challenge that you are not able to handle, it's a good idea to pray more often. Thank Hashem for all the good he has provided. You can even make a deal with Hashem. Take something upon yourself. It doesn't have to be a drastic move. Give charity, say an extra chapter of Tehilim, or ask Hashem for help. You can't serve Hashem conditionally; you should pray with unconditional love. Sometimes it may seem like Hashem is not living up to His part of the deal. That's where faith comes in. Hashem knows what He is doing and accepts all prayers. Only He knows the big picture and understands all. Humans are just mortals with limited intelligence, and it's not our place to question Hashem. He knows what He is doing. No matter how bleak a situation may appear, try to have faith. Appreciate all your gifts – from health to wealth to all areas of your life. It's not easy, but if you make a deal with Hashem, you will grow.[77] The "Let's Make a Deal" approach acknowledges that you are aware that it is only Hashem that can help. At the right time, He will reciprocate in more ways than you ever imagined.

Love, Daddy

STRIVE FOR EXCELLENCE

"If one wants to understand his mission, he must discover his weakness and attempt to strengthen it."

My Dear Children,

Nothing makes me prouder than your success. Becoming successful is not easy. It requires discipline, personal sacrifice, faith, constant perseverance, tenacity, and the drive to do your best.[78] In order to succeed in business, building a family, investing in spirituality, fitness, or anything that you are striving for, the challenge is resisting the Yetzer Hara. All you must do is realize your weaknesses and construct a plan to become stronger. As in all things that are important, prayer and faith are essential. It takes time. Just keep going, day by day, and keep growing. Do this and you'll be able to resist the Yetzer Hara, thus winning the battle. You may lose a few rounds, but keep getting back up for another. Have faith in Hashem, because most of all, He wants you to "Strive for Excellence" to receive your ultimate reward.

Love, Daddy

GOSSIP IS THE ENEMY

"One word can change a person's life forever."

My Dear Children,

As soldiers of Hashem, we might have to go to war, metaphorically speaking. When you have a disagreement with someone, please try to control your tongue. You may want to say something in the heat of battle, but please try to resist. Angry and mean words are very difficult to take back. People are sensitive. Today, it's easy to insult someone or spread evil gossip. With social media and texting, it's exceedingly easy to express your feelings without confrontation. A few years ago, we would have had to have a conversation, either face-to-face or on the phone. Today, one email or text can destroy everything. We all have this tremendous power to anonymously hurt others. That's why it's so important to think carefully before speaking, especially when we're angry. The power of self-control is most rewarding. Please realize that Hashem gave you speech so that you could utter words of encouragement, love, and closeness to one another. Our words should be used to praise Hashem's miracles. Prayer is the greatest way to use our words, and gossip is the worst.[79] Spirituality and prayer create self-control. "Gossip Is the Enemy" of man. Please use the gift of speech to elevate Hashem's blessings to the world.

Love, Daddy

HASHEM'S NO FLY ZONE

"A vacuum of spirituality is an open wound of the soul."

My Dear Children,

Most parents have issues with the rising costs of tuition, but truthfully, it's an everlasting investment. A formal Jewish education sets up a foundation of tradition, community, and love for your fellow man. Charity teaches us the value of kindness. We learn that when one Jew suffers, we all suffer; and when one rejoices, we all rejoice. The educational foundation is a template set up for you and your children. Instead of complaining about tuition, say thank you to Hashem. A Jewish education maintains our religious traditions. If you're ever feeling empty, please avoid dangerous situations and people. Stay true to who you are. Do not succumb to peer pressure. The Torah is set up to implement rules and regulations. Surround yourself with good people, friends, and family. Be careful where you send your children to school. Watch them and protect them from intruders and others who may not share your spiritual values.[80] Pray for protection from atmospheres that can compromise "Hashem's No Fly Zone", since it's a place where you don't belong.

Love, Daddy

ONE DAY AT A TIME

"A goal of the evil inclination is to cause confusion of the mind."

My Dear Children,

During your lifetime, you will experience the loss of someone you really love.[81] My strongest prayers are that they should be natural losses – no tragedies. During the challenge, please connect to Hashem with prayer and faith. Donate money in the person's merit. Talk about him and how much he meant to you. Some people hide their feelings, as they are too painful to discuss. That's okay, but I truly believe it is healthy to express how you feel. If the loss is overwhelming, my best advice is to take it one day at a time. The Jewish process of one-year of mourning is brilliant. You will have good days and bad days. The evil inclination will try to throw you into despair, please don't give into it. You will have your moments. It is taking many years to mourn the loss of Jerusalem, but we believe that Jerusalem will be rebuilt. The "One Day at a Time" approach rebuilds all broken hearts.

Love, Daddy

SPIRITUAL LANDSCAPING

"One's evil inclination is the best motivator for personal and spiritual growth."

My Dear Children,

During successful years, don't let the grass grow under your feet. It causes laziness and lack of productivity. Always look for the next step, the next opportunity.[82] This doesn't only apply to business, but also to your emotional and spiritual goals. Study the teachings of our Rabbis and learn about how they conducted their lives. Reflect on Hashem's kindness to you and your family. To maintain a growth pattern, always have a routine. Without a routine a person lacks structure. He lacks the foundation to maintain his balance in challenging times. If a person is stagnant in his growth, actually moving backwards, then he is inviting the evil inclination into his life. It causes boredom, which can lead to nonproductive results. In business, a stagnant person can lose his place in the market and his competition. Man was created to stand on his feet and to grow daily. However, one's evil inclination can be one's greatest asset. It causes him to constantly fight against it. The evil inclination will send you obstacles that you will have to overcome, and once you are successful, it will constantly challenge you. During this battle, you will become stronger every day. If an obstacle is too tough, pray to Hashem to help you and make it easier. Ask Hashem to send you the tools to keep your landscape clean. Constantly reflecting and taking inventory are great tools for "Spiritual Landscaping."

Love, Daddy

THE PERFECT STORM

"Man must do his work to till the earth; faith and prayer are the facilitators of all blessings."

My Dear Children,

When you're doing well and living comfortably, your life can be affected by the changing economy, or some other situation that you can't control. During these times, the way you react is crucial. Please realize that, as always, it is Hashem who is preparing you for your next level of greatness. It may feel like a storm – overwhelming – and that is where faith comes in. It would be easy for Hashem to fix your situation, yet he may cause it to worsen. A person with faith will see this as an opportunity to improve his situation. Use your G-d given talents to enhance your career and make it even better than it was before. With faith, please believe that Hashem is performing "The Perfect Storm" for your ultimate perfection.[83]

Love, Daddy

THE KING'S HIGHWAY

"A routine of prayer, learning, and faith maintains healthy spiritual highways."

My Dear Children,

There are few things more important than your physical health. Exercise and proper diet are crucial. Always look your best, even when you are not feeling great. The way you look on the outside can cause your inside to feel better. However, you are not only a physical being. One of the few things more important than your physical health is your spiritual well-being. Torah learning, self-growth books, and giving to charities all help nourish the health of your soul. When you eat well, your body will respond accordingly. If you eat unhealthy foods, it can, G-d forbid, cause heart issues. The same is true for spirituality. When you nourish yourself with kosher surroundings, friends, and learning, your soul will respond accordingly. A negative environment can harm your soul. So please be careful not to get involved with anyone or anything that can lead you away from your religion or otherwise compromise your connection to Hashem. The physical pipes are the arteries and veins that transport blood from the heart.[84] We also need clean spiritual pipes to go up "The King's Highway" to feed and nourish your soul. This will lead to happiness and connection to Hashem.

Love, Daddy

THE ALARM CLOCK OF GUILT

"The feeling of guilt is an antibody to heal a spiritual wound."

My Dear Children,

Nobody is perfect. The key is how you respond to sin. Hashem created man with a fantastic trait – we feel guilty after we do something wrong. There may be a time when you commit a transgression and feel badly about it. That feeling comes from Hashem to get you back on track. Guilt gives you the power to realize your fault and confess. If you do this, Hashem will accept your plea.[85] Hashem is all about kindness and will forgive you and wipe the slate clean. However, if you don't pay attention to the guilt and repeat that transgression repeatedly, the guilt can wear off. Once the guilt is gone, the act becomes acceptable to you. This can lead to more transgression and sever one's connection to Hashem. If this ever happens to you, please pray and invest more time into spiritual growth. Please imitate the traits of Hashem – help others, be kind, and invest your time reconnecting with Him. Guilt can also work in the reverse. It can cause a person to lose hope in himself and, G-d forbid, abandon his faith. A person in that state should realize that Hashem never abandons his children, and the door to repentance is always open. When the "Alarm Clock of Guilt" rings, thank Hashem, as He is asking you to return home.

Love, Daddy

THE LONGEST YARD

"To score a personal touchdown, one has to be in fantastic mental shape."

My Dear Children,

There are times you should thank Hashem for the evil inclination because it is meant to challenge and strengthen you.[86] Each day the evil inclination puts together a strategy to weaken you. When you don't let this happen, you move closer to your goals. Always fight against it, especially during challenging times. With each day of fighting back, you are getting stronger. When you are closest to your goals, the resistance gets tougher, until you finally end up at the goal with a touchdown. One of the most fundamental traits to have during challenging times is faith in Hashem through prayer and learning. Have confidence in yourself and never give up. You may get tackled here and there, but never take your eye off the goal post. Never look back; always move forward. If you feel you need help, turn to a Rabbi or mentor; they are your coaches. There will be times when you don't score a touchdown. Just have faith and always keep learning and growing. Keep fighting. The final battle can be "The Longest Yard" to a touchdown!

Love, Daddy

PART 7

THE SEVENTH HIGHWAY OF THE SOUL: HOME SWEET HOME

March 2011 - Present

Now that I was comfortable in my own home, life became very steady. After being on the road for close to 12 years, I found myself very comfortable in a steady routine. I was finally able to come home, cook myself dinner, watch a TV show, and go to sleep. Life became calm and easy. My kids were doing great. My apartment was one block from the synagogue, and I was three blocks from the train to NYC. Life became convenient and easy. However, too easy can cause boredom. I started to study foreign ideologies and challenged it with Judaism. The pull towards California was starting to gnaw at me again. However, Hashem took over and showed me point blank, that foreign ideologies were not the way to go. Prayer and connection to my children and my community planted my feet. After that final battle, I was introduced to my wife, and we were married. Hashem blessed us. We have two kids together. With my new life, I am thankful to Hashem for sending us continued blessings. I had many choices and I had to learn the hard way to earn blessing. Once a person is secure and safe in his home, Hashem reciprocates with more blessings. After completing this Journey of 16 years, I appreciate my "Home Sweet Home."

The final letters are the last bits of advice I have for you, for now. No matter what life throws your way, when you stay true to you and Hashem, all will be well.

COMFORT ZONES

"Taking one out of a comfort zone is melting away the ice of one's winter to prepare for his springtime."

My Dear Children,

As children you were always fed, dressed and taken care of. As parents we did everything to ensure your comfort.[87] As you grow older, you must emerge from that comfort zone of dependency and become responsible for yourself. Even though you may feel alone, your parents are always there to guide and protect you, even if you don't see it. At first it will be difficult leaving the comfort of your parents, but it is an essential part of your growth and survival. Appreciate the comfort you were given, and most of all, express your gratitude to Hashem for His guidance.

During your career, and in your personal life, things may feel robotic and redundant. When this happens, it's time to look for the next step in your journey. Start by investing your time in learning, praying, working, and most importantly, growing with your family. If you don't, you'll stay stagnant, which can cause a lot of frustration. If you are in such a situation, design a plan to carve yourself out of the robotic comfort zone you're in. Pray to Hashem and have faith that He will rescue you at the right time. It may not happen overnight, so please don't be impulsive. Patience is key. The evil inclination wants to keep you knee deep where you are, and create a false sense of security, since it is afraid you will grow. Daily introspection and talking to a Rabbi or mentor will always help. Have faith that just as your parents will always be there for you, so will Hashem. He will orchestrate your freedom, either directly or behind the scenes, to rescue you from the slavery of a complacent "Comfort Zone."

Love, Daddy

FEAR FACTOR

"When a person is filled with fear and love for someone, he imitates their actions."

My Dear Children,

One of the first things we learn as a child is to fear Hashem.[88] However, fear in any relationship really doesn't work. Performing tasks out of fear of punishment is a slave mentality and not healthy. It is not a way to build any kind of relationship – with Hashem or any human being. We should love Hashem because He is a supreme being who can change anything at any time. Being in awe of another human being creates respect. It could be a Rabbi, friend, or elderly person. Hashem wants us to love and respect Him out of love and be in awe of His greatness. Sometimes you may love someone, but fearing them could be dangerous. Insecure and controlling people intimidate others to cause fear. Never, ever, fear any individual who is trying to control you. If you are in such a situation, pray to Hashem to rescue you. Express your love to Him. Faith in Hashem will take the "Fear Factor" away.

Love, Daddy

STAGES OF REDEMPTION

"Challenges are Hashem's way of setting up the process of redemption."

My Dear Children,

You will always have your share of challenges. Please don't fall into despair and hopelessness. It is often the result of lack of faith in Hashem. It is the job of the evil inclination to bring you down to surrender. The art of Judaism and its teachings is the key to turning a challenge into redemption. It is a time for introspection, prayer, and faith that Hashem will rescue you at the right time. Today, we live in a quick fix generation. Please remember, a quick fix is a band-aid. In the short term you may feel accomplished, but it lacks any sort of foundation for future redemption.[89] When our ancestors left Egypt, they were saved in stages. Once you take the initiative to change a negative trait and confront it, Hashem will take you into His arms and lead you towards your goal. If it takes time, you are on the right path. Just be patient. Follow the rules and you will change your "Stages of Redemption" to your Ultimate Redemption.

Love, Daddy

NOURISHMENT OF THE SOUL

"The soul is given a mission in a physical body to accomplish in this world which then bridges to the next world."

My Dear Children,

As you grow older you will realize that the material life is just a façade. It is okay to want good things. A nice car, a house, and money are always great. But they can also be dangerous. You will need spirituality and connection to Hashem to appreciate them. We all have a drive to want more, and you are entitled to it, and that should be channeled in the appropriate direction. However, it shouldn't take over your spirituality. Physical cravings have their limitations, but spirituality lasts forever. Develop a relationship with Hashem by taking an account of your week, month, or year. Give charity, perform good deeds, and help others. Always express gratitude to Hashem, especially during challenging times.[90] Do not be a prisoner of your personal cravings! Use your gift of speech to praise others. If you are upset, try to control your anger and learn the value of peace of mind. You need humility to be able to appreciate the small things in life. There are many distractions, but you should fight them with prayer and learning proper character traits. It's a lifelong battle. The physical body is just a costume, one that you are obligated to take care of; however, the "Nourishment of the Soul" is everlasting.

Love, Daddy

THE GOOD EARTH

"No matter how successful we are, it is Hashem who is responsible for our good fortune."

My Dear Children,

Humans arrive on this earth from dust. Therefore, you should be humble. Humble yourself before Hashem and thank Him for all you have.[91] Our nation was built on gratitude and humility. However, please realize that soil brings food to billions of people. It gives forth fruit and nourishment. We plant a seed in the ground and an apple tree and flowers grow. The abundance of worldly supply of food nourishes the entire planet.

Inside every human being is a seed of creative talent for success. It could be sales, marketing, shipping, teaching, learning, writing, etc. The key is to use that talent to do good and also for your livelihood. Then, thank Hashem with humility for those gifts. Whatever Hashem gives you, thank Him and always tell others it is from Him. Perform acts of kindness, give charity, and help others! Keep your head down in humility and at the same time, feel confident that you can achieve success with your talents. Learn from the "Good Earth"; learn that you are created from dust within the soil, and it is the creativity specially crafted for your success.

Love, Daddy

NECESSARY BALANCES

"Prayer has the power of a sword to cut through the toughest of challenges."

My Dear Children,

Everything in life needs balance. During your journey, please notice that as strong as you are getting, in every area of growth, there is a gravitational pull to try and weaken you. When you conquer the challenge, you will become stronger. When you lose a challenge, you will not get weaker if you get up and learn from the experience and start over. Don't let technology distract you. Our world is moving at an incredible pace. With technology, one touch of a button and the world is at your fingertips. Technology has its benefits, but it can very easily cause distraction. Multi-tasking can cause you to lose focus. A person can spend hours on social media without even realizing how much time he has wasted. Please balance your time to focus on connecting to Hashem through prayer, concentrating on your work, and investing your time with your family.[92] We love the convenience of technology, but we need "Necessary Balances" to achieve greatness.

Love, Daddy

Spiritual Life Insurance

"Appreciating parents, grandparents, and the elderly is our gift."

My Dear Children,

Did you ever wonder why you are so lucky to live in a secluded community? Do you appreciate the lifestyle and support available? Outside communities must fend for themselves with little support from their neighbors. The bottom line is we are all living on our grandparent's and ancestor's merits. They spent countless hours praying for future generations to maintain their lifestyle, to live separately, and serve each other.[93] It is a great gift and a life insurance policy to protect our pedigree. Please imitate your grandparents and pray for your children and future grandchildren. They need it, especially with today's social influences. Please don't take for granted how lucky you are - appreciate it! Hashem's kindness in response to prayer has set up a foundation to maintain our legacy. Even though it is extremely expensive, the best insurance policy is educating the youth and teaching them proper character traits. However, there are times that a child or an adult might stumble off the path. Nobody really leaves the confines of a comfortable, supportive community on purpose. Try to help anyone who is on a path to leave the community. The greatest asset is the "Spiritual Life Insurance" invested to perpetuate your legacy.

Love, Daddy

ALL FOR ONE

"A Torah-based life arms us with stingers of protection against alien philosophies."

My Dear Children,

One of the most precious gifts you have is the community you live in. If you ever have an issue or a challenge, the community is always there – spiritually, physically and financially. Please don't take it for granted. You are blessed! Our institutions perpetuate our legacy. Most of all, stay united for this purpose. Please don't let your ego ever get in the way. It all comes from Hashem. Ego is a mechanism of the evil inclination to divide a community or an institution within a community. Listen to the Rabbi or leader of the organization you belong to. He knows best. Always ask for his advice. Don't let petty arguments upset you. Rabbis and leaders should not be there for their own aggrandizement. They should be humble and act in the interest of the community and as a servant of Hashem. Try to avoid the leaders who have inflated egos, as it could disturb their judgment. Most of all, keep your family, friends, and peers close to you. Don't sweat the small stuff! Rise above it, because it's all petty. Appreciate what you have and thank Hashem through prayer. Use your talents to serve the community and assist others. This is an "All for One" attitude to maintain the survival of your family and community.[94]

Love, Daddy

RESISTANCE TRAINING

"Resistance training is a necessary ingredient towards success."

My Dear Children,

Challenges are often perceived as major inconveniences. This is not so. Challenge is a gift that leads to growth. When faced with a challenge, thank Hashem for it.[95] He is preparing you for the next chapter in your journey of growth. Resistance is healthy, but you must balance it by considering the big picture and discovering what is really happening. You can face tests of resistance in almost every part of your life: in relationships, employment, religion, etc. The key is to know when to stay and fight for what you want and when to walk away. If you are feeling anxious, uptight, confused or obsessive, it is Hashem telling you it is not healthy. Trust your gut and construct an exit plan from the situation. However, if you feel yourself becoming mentally stronger and sharper, it means the challenge is important and will lead to growth. Nothing worth having comes easily. So please keep up the great work and keep growing. If you are not sure whether the situation is good for you, ask a Rabbi or close friend for advice. Pray and have trust that if you are doing the right thing, Hashem will help you. "Resistance Training" is your pathway to what really matters and will help you win the battle against the evil inclination inside of you.

Love, Daddy

HITTING THE JACKPOT

"Every vice is tailor made for each person."

My Dear Children,

One of the most challenging addictions is gambling. The evil one works very cleverly with this disease.[96] The first time you visit a casino, you might win. Once you win, all the bells and atmosphere can lure you back. Before you know it, you will lose a few hands of Blackjack or a couple rolls of the dice. Then you'll want to play more to recover your losses. The best scenario is the first time you enter a casino, you lose, and the next time, you lose again. This is Hashem's kindness. When you lose, it may feel unlucky, but it also makes it less appealing. You probably won't want to return for a long time. One can become addicted to many things: gambling, drinking, smoking, drugs, and the desire for immorality. These are all taking a gamble on ruining your life. They are the vehicles of the evil inclination, which is out to destroy you and your family. There is nothing wrong with an occasional drink or roll of the dice. The detriment is when these things become important, and you can't stop thinking about them. Pace yourself and know your limits.

If, G-d forbid, you find yourself in an addictive situation, seek help. Quitting an addiction is almost impossible to do by yourself. You need a support system. A Rabbi, mentor, a close friend, or a support group can assist you. When you win at gambling, and money comes too easily, it causes a lack of appreciation of G-d's benevolence. A slow nickel is better than a fast dollar. Working for your money leads to stability and discipline. Please take constant inventory of your life and appreciate Hashem's gifts to you every day. Once you create the habit of introspection, you will thank Hashem for letting you "Hit the Jackpot" without walking into a casino.

Love, Daddy

MIND CONTROL

"Pure thoughts are required to keep the mind in healthy condition."

My Dear Children,

Computers are imitations of the human mind. Your mind is one of Hashem's greatest gifts. It is your responsibility to keep your mind pure and clear. While you're alive, everything you see, hear, smell, taste, and touch is downloaded into your brain. And everything downloaded produces a reaction – positive or negative. To keep things positive, you must keep your mind healthy. This happens when you're around positive people and thoughts, and when you're learning and growing spiritually. The mind, like a computer, is very prone to viruses that can lead to a crash. A negative atmosphere can poison the mind and corrupt the internal hard drive.[97] However, unlike a computer that crashes beyond recovery, the human mind can recover through the fantastic gift of returning to Hashem and a healthy atmosphere. That is the teshuva process. It's an open miracle when the mind recovers from illness. A person must take the first step through prayer and connecting to Hashem. Please, thank Hashem daily for the gift of a healthy mind, and make sure that your environment is positive, as this is the best preventive medicine to maintain proper "Mind Control."

Love, Daddy

CONCENTRATION, LOVE, AND FAITH

"Shabbat is the best day to praise and thank Hashem for His kindness."

My Dear Children,

One of the most effective ways to get what you want out of life is to focus on your end goal. Pray and have faith that Hashem will assist you. Study and read books on faith and appreciation of Hashem's love for you.[98] Take on something simple to show Hashem your desire to reach your goal and concentrate on what you need to do to accomplish it. Today, we are blessed with amazing technology, which can be used to learn anything you choose to study. Unfortunately, that same technology can distract you from achieving your goals. It is a tool of the evil inclination to keep a person so busy with frivolous things that he doesn't strive for his goals. Pray to Hashem to help you use technology to achieve your dreams and to get closer to Him. You can channel your distraction to "Concentration, Love, and Faith" in Hashem, which will bring you closer to your goals.

Love, Daddy

Our mother synagogue in Brooklyn

A TREE THAT GREW IN BROOKLYN

"Surrounding ourselves with spirituality creates a healthy branch on a tree."

My Dear Children,

Think of life like a tree: The seeds you plant will eventually grow into a tree that will bear fruit that will be distributed to others.[99] You are responsible for planting the seeds you wish to grow. As a child, you grew up in a religious community. The proper seeds were planted in you to produce a productive life. The distribution of the fruit you bear is entirely up to your free choice. As you become a parent, please plant the right seeds into your children. A Torah-based life, with fear and love of Hashem, is a life of bearing and giving fruit, not taking. This will lead to a life of maintaining the proper atmosphere of community and peers; a life of spreading peace and love. Please avoid the toxic atmosphere dictated by society. Please avoid negative, ruinous people who can suppress your confidence and ridicule your desire to grow. Rotten fruit can hurt the tree and eventually damage the roots that were planted centuries ago. Pray to Hashem to protect you from bad influences. Pray for the confidence in yourself to know when to turn away from a situation that can end up risky. Trust your gut; it never lies! A life of spiritual growth lasts forever. Even a small "Tree that Grew in Brooklyn" can grow to be a life-giving tree benefitting society.

Love, Daddy

LIFE CHANGES IN THE BLINK OF AN EYE

"One's spiritual camera must be focused on faith in Hashem."

My Dear Children,

There are times that your life can change in an instant. One minute you will feel totally in control, and the next everything will seem unbalanced.[100] It could be a job promotion, purchasing a home, or a challenging situation. That is the way Hashem works; you can never understand His ways, because you are only human. With that in mind, you will have to adjust accordingly. Because you grew up in this amazing community, received a religious education, have so many people who support and love you, you should be able to go with the flow and adjust readily. Due to your solid foundation and spirituality, a compromising situation may put a dent in the foundation, but it will not cause your entire life to come crumbling down. And in time, G-d willing, you will fully adjust and return to a new routine. Having humility and faith in Hashem's plan is tough, but essential during challenging times. A person without a solid connection to Hashem will have a much tougher time. He may turn to quick fixes to try and alleviate the pressure. The ultimate adjustment is realizing that Hashem is in control and although "Life Changes in the Blink of an Eye" it is for your own good and for your growth. I have no doubt that you can handle any situation that comes along.

Love, Daddy

FROM PERIL TO PROTECTION
"Prayers cause us to acknowledge that Hashem is our only protector."

My Dear Children,

Always remember that Hashem is protecting you, through good times and bad. It's important to have faith.[101] Some people are not aware of this, so it's important to pray for them. However, don't pray for selfish reasons. Pray because you sincerely care about the person in need. When you pray for others, they may never know it was your prayer that helped them out of a tough situation. Praying for others forms an everlasting bond between you and the person you pray for, and it also creates a bond between you and Hashem. He loves when you care for others without an ulterior motive. Hashem, in His kindness and His infinite wisdom, gives you the opportunity to pray for others, to build your account of merits. Often, a person could be headed for a perilous situation. It could be your prayer, sensitivity, or comforting words and support that change his destiny. If you know someone in trouble, try to assist. The only time you should not try to help him is when it compromises your safety, which should always come first. Know when to help and when to walk away. Try to always have a positive outlook on life. It will help in your personal, financial, and spiritual growth. A positive attitude will help you approach the right people when you need advice. The right friends can shift a person "From Peril to Protection" into Hashem's loving arms.

Love, Daddy

MAINTAINING YOUR SPIRITUAL HEALTH

"Introspection and confession brings us closer to Hashem."

My Dear Children,

Eating lots of vegetables, fruits, and other foods high in vitamins and minerals is vital to maintain your physical health. However, caring for your spiritual health is equally, if not more, essential. Praying and appreciating Hashem's kindness is crucial to your faith and spiritual well-being. Please be kind to others and remain humble. After a transgression towards Hashem or your fellow man, apologize. Don't let pride get in the way. Always take responsibility for your mistakes, because arrogance and pride are antithetical to your spiritual health. When you admit that you are wrong, you will be forgiven. Even if you believe that you are right, but it's hurting your relationship, apologize! It will bring you closer to the person you disagree with, and closer to Hashem. Once you take responsibility, you are given a clean slate to begin again. Starting over is a great process, as you know what to avoid in the future. And just as you want to be forgiven for your transgressions, always forgive others, as it is not healthy to hold a grudge.[102] Even if you are right, your humility will be recognized and will help you in the process of "Maintaining Your Spiritual Health."

Love, Daddy

THE ATTITUDE OF GRATITUDE

"The nest of the world is constructed to be tailor made for man."

My Dear Children,

One of the first lessons we learn in life is to say thank you when you're given a gift, and when someone says something nice to you. It's a lesson that is just as valuable in adulthood. Expressing gratitude shows that you truly appreciate and value the people in your life and, of course, Hashem.[103] Today, many people are not happy. One of the reasons for this is that they are good people, but they are not appreciated for the good they do. This is due to dealing with others that are ingrates. Being unappreciative towards others is a terrible character trait. It denotes arrogance and the feeling of entitlement. You should never take anyone or anything for granted. Being thankful creates bonds of friendship. Our prayers begin with gratitude and move on to requests. Before you ask for something from anyone, thank him first. We tend to thank Hashem for the big blessings he bestows on us, but it's just as important to thank Him for the little things in life, because it shows that we know He is responsible for everything – big and small. The "Attitude of Gratitude" will cause Hashem to shower blessings upon you and your family. Amen!

Love, Daddy

THE SPIRITUAL HURRICANE

"The heavens respond to man's actions on earth."

My Dear Children,

It is easy to be good to others when things are calm and peaceful. The test of loyalty arrives in times of crisis. This is what separates true friends from fair weather friends.[104] True friends are supportive, stay with you, and offer help in times of need. Fair weather friends take off the moment things start getting difficult. It's important to be a good friend. It's okay to be picky when it comes to friends. You don't have to be friends with everyone; however, when you do care for someone, show them your appreciation and stay loyal to them. If you witness a friend going through his own "hurricane" please assist him. Most people can survive a physical hurricane. The danger is that the emotional and physical impact can hurt his spirituality and closeness to Hashem. A spiritual malady can be worse than a physical or monetary issue. A person with damaged faith can lose his spirituality forever. Don't let that happen. Hashem loves when you are a good friend and help others, especially when there's nothing for you to gain from it. This is the key to selflessness. Thank Hashem for giving you the strength to assist others in their times of need. Physical hurricanes get repaired in time. Kindness, faith, and connection to Hashem help us avoid "Spiritual Hurricanes."

Love, Daddy

AWAKENINGS

"During sleep our souls arrive at a station in heaven for a replenishment of energy."

My Dear Children,

After a long day, your body needs rest and sleep. During sleep, your body is parked at a fuel station where renewed energy is pumped for the next day. You awake revitalized, and ready to tackle new challenges and opportunities. Always thank Hashem for your renewed spirit and energy.[105] If, one day, you awake feeling lethargic and you don't want to get out of bed, it's time to take inventory of your daily routine and try to pinpoint the area depleting your fuel supply. Pay attention to the atmosphere around you to determine if it is healthy. Determine if it's a relationship that's getting you down. Pray and connect to Hashem, and reach out to a Rabbi or friend for help. While trying to find the issue that's sapping your energy, eat right, exercise, continue learning Torah, and pray to Hashem. Faith and prayer beget positive results. Seek help if needed, until you find the cause of your distress, and then do your best to fix the issue. Hopefully, this won't happen. Create a healthy environment with a positive group of friends and you will experience "Awakenings" of spirit, everyday.

Love, Daddy

A BALANCED BUDGET

"Our ammunition to change a situation is humility, repentance, and prayer."

My Dear Children,

Life is like a savings account where all the positive things you have, like a stable marriage, a secure job, an actual bank account, discipline, prayer, and kindness equal deposits. In a spiritual sense, there is no such thing as a bad economy. Even if you hit a rough patch, and perhaps lose your job for a little while, remember, if you continue to pray, and be a dependable and kind person, these things will go into a perpetual savings account. You, along with your wife, children, and many future generations can live off those dividends. It's a win/win situation. Please make daily deposits into your relationship with your spouse, children, family, friends and community. Your character is a huge deposit, as is being an excellent role model for others. The most effective way to maintain "A Balanced Budget" is having humility, repenting when necessary, and praying on a regular basis. That is the best insurance policy you can have for your spiritual bank account.[106]

Love, Daddy

BITTERSWEET

"Food and its nutritional value are everyday miracles that take place right before our eyes."

My Dear Children,

Sometimes you might need a little bitterness in your life to appreciate the blessings. The key is to remain faithful in Hashem's service with prayer. One doesn't become successful overnight. It takes years of hard work and dedication. Quick fixes don't work. It's about consistency and continual introspection. There may be times when your day to day life seems overwhelming and feels hopeless – so much so that you question Hashem, and G-d forbid, disconnect from your family and community. Please, whatever you are going through, I implore you to never give up hope. Pray to Hashem, connect to a Rabbi, confide in your spouse, and remember that I'm always here for you. Think about how your ancestors survived persecution for 2,000 years. They managed to remain hopeful through the most terrible times. So, when things seem overwhelming, pray and take things one day at a time. Do everything you can to remain faithful. Then, when things get better, and they will, you'll appreciate the good so much more. You will notice that the waters that were bitter have become "Bittersweet".[107]

Love, Daddy

ABOVE THE CLOUDS

"All prayers are stored in a spiritual cloud drive."

My Dear Children,

Computers were created to make life easier. They can store billions of files of memory. With recent technological advances, files are even stored in a cloud. The brain, like a computer, stores countless bits of information from the minute you were born, and these files from your lifetime can be accessed at any time. One of the miracles of the brain is its ability to forget. If it weren't for the wonder of forgetfulness, we would not be able to move on after a stressful situation. If someone ever hurts your feelings, or does something very bad to you, please try to forget about it and forgive him. It will take a lot of pride and strength, but your brain doesn't need to hold onto those files. I am not advising you to be his/her best friend, but try to use the art of forgetfulness to move on. Take the higher ground and let go of pride, anger, and jealousy. If you find this difficult, pray to Hashem to help you. Like your computer, your prayers are stored somewhere safe, where they are held until Hashem is ready to answer them. Sometimes your prayers may seem denied, but please have the faith that your prayer is stored "Above the Clouds" to be answered from Hashem in heaven, when He knows the time is right.[108]

Love, Daddy

RESTRICTIONS ARE PRESCRIPTIONS

"A Torah-based life is a prescription for spiritual and physical health."

My Dear Children,

You should thank Hashem daily for placing you in a community of religion, tradition, and a Torah-based life. Just as preventive medicine keeps you healthy, a Torah-based life keeps you from permitting the negative influences of the outside world to enter your life. Restrictions from eating certain foods, not working on Shabbat, and the command to fast for a few days of the year may seem like a burden at times; however, it is like a vaccination or a cure before the sickness.[109] We have 613 commandments: 365 negative commandments and 248 positive ones. Each time we perform a good deed, it affects our bodies spiritually and physically. Unfortunately, the opposite is also true. There are times it might appear restrictive to hear, "No, you can't do it! You are not allowed!" Try not to let it upset you, because it's Hashem's directions you are following, just as you would follow the rules of a protective parent. Please realize that restraint is the cure! Hashem, in His kindness, knows what is best for you and wants you physically and spiritually healthy. Having all you want in this world is not freedom. It can, G-d forbid, lead to unsavory practices and even addiction, which is slavery and confining! Living a Torah-based life is your passage to personal and spiritual freedom. Remember, "Restrictions Are Prescriptions."

Love, Daddy

LIFE IS A BALLGAME

"Faith, perseverance, and proper training create a strategy for victory."

My Dear Children,

Watching sports is a great American hobby for many people. It can be exciting to watch your favorite team win. A team wins a ballgame not because of one person's home run, but because of the synergy of everyone on the team.[110] Everyday is another ballgame. As you are geared for success, there may be obstacles in your path. One of the major lessons we can learn from a winning team is the value of teamwork. In business and your personal life, it is important to help others and work with them to create success. Very few people can do it alone. Working with others towards a common goal is a great gift of synergy. Always maintain a healthy, positive atmosphere. Please, always make sure you are exceptionally close to your family, peers, and community. Praying together in a minyan invites the Divine Presence. Hashem loves to see His children working and praying together. Pray to Hashem for the right team to work with. Remember "Life Is a Ballgame" and please use your talents to work with others towards a common goal, so that you can share in the success!

Love, Daddy

BEHIND THE CURTAINS

"Each person has been created with a specific role in his own movie."

My Dear Children,

As you proceed on your life's journey, remember that you are being guided by Hashem.[111] In the background, everything is being orchestrated for your ultimate success. All you must do is pay attention to the details. Reflecting on the miracle of the human body helps you connect to Hashem. Things cannot work without a conductor or a captain. Hashem is always in the background. If you are living a life of faith, prayer, and spirituality, you will recognize Hashem's miracles. For anything successful to occur, lots of things must click. When you are working on business deals, many things are happening in the background to bring them to a successful outcome. Just reflect on how many things must go right, simultaneously, from an idea to a product selling on the retail floor. On the other hand, those who do not see Hashem in the background are not as connected. They leave things to nature, chance, and coincidence. They fail to see the wonderful orchestration of their Creator. Living with faith and prayer increases your gratitude and appreciation of Hashem's kindness. It will bring you continued blessing and success. Recognizing Hashem "Behind the Curtains" will eventually help you see His miracles directly and His continued involvement in your life.

Love, Daddy

LOST AND FOUND

"Our family, friends, and community have a responsibility to make sure our children never get lost."

My Dear Children,

During challenging times you may feel lost, and that can cause you to withdraw from religion. Whatever your challenge, there is always a solution. No matter how lost you may feel, never forget who you are! Your self-confidence and integrity should never be compromised. As your confidence increases, your humility should increase as well. Humility will cause you to appreciate Hashem and His kindness towards you. An antidote to feeling lost is appreciation for the things you usually take for granted. You are so very lucky to be part of a community that is equipped with many organizations that exist solely to help community members with all types of issues. Often, a person who is experiencing a problem needs someone who understands to discuss the issue at hand. During these times, don't ever feel embarrassed by asking for help. That's why the community organizations are there. They truly want to help, and see you succeed.[112] You, too, should try to help others when they're in need, whether they need a job, advice or just a friend to talk to. Try not to reject anyone, because when a person in need feels a sense of rejection, he is in danger of getting lost. He may leave our secure community. You never know how just listening might assist others. If you are not able to help him, refer him to someone who can. Hashem loves when you care for others. Above all, faith and prayer will have a "Lost and Found" result on you and anyone you assist.

Love, Daddy

TRAFFIC OF THE MIND

"A clear mind is focused and free of traffic."

My Dear Children,

There will always be challenges in your life. They may come in business, financial dealings, or in a relationship. Always have faith that Hashem will assist you; however, you must do your part as well. Put in the effort. Try to spend less time obsessing about the situation, and more time assessing it. Obsession causes confusion and it is a vehicle to keep you distracted from focusing on the possibilities at hand. If you find yourself obsessing about the situation, take a break. Go for a walk, exercise, or read a book. Tune out all distractions like technology. Also, take advantage of Shabbat, which is a gift to relax your mind and help you let go of life's distractions. Speak to a Rabbi or mentor to assist you and help you proceed in the proper direction. It is very difficult to fix any sort of problem by yourself. It's important to know that the problem will not go away overnight. It could take a while; please be patient. Staying on the right path and keeping a clear mind will eventually cause a ripple effect, and G-d willing, you will see a turnaround.[113] During confusing times, please remain steadfast in your spirituality and connection to Hashem. When you have faith in Hashem, you're able to see His miracles. Distraction causes "Traffic of the Mind." Faith and prayer will give you clarity of mind.

Love, Daddy

THE FINISH LINE

"In order to grow, one's physical and spiritual muscles must be fatigued."

My Dear Children,

You were not sent to this world to have a life without resistance. You were sent here with a mission, along with G-d given talents to accomplish it. It is one of the fundamental keys to maintaining your self-confidence along with gratitude and humility towards Hashem. As you approach a goal, don't be surprised if there are potholes and hurdles. Please don't be discouraged if you fall. The essential part is getting as far as you did towards your goal. Please don't listen to your inner voice that will try to make you feel unaccomplished. It's not true! Hashem considers all your efforts worthwhile. Life is not always about winning! Continue to pray to Hashem with a happy heart, and He will continue to give you the tools you'll need to accomplish your mission.[114] When you find something very challenging, think of it as Hashem advising you that you can do better, to motivate you to work harder and train more effectively so that you will eventually reach your goal. If you ever fall short of your mission, please thank Hashem for the opportunity you were given, and the talents He has given you. The next time, you will cross "The Finish Line" and train others to do the same.

Love, Daddy

THE ENERGY OF THE HEART

"Receiving words of encouragement will revitalize you and bypass any negative blood flow to your heart."

My Dear Children,

Proper nutrition and exercise have a positive impact on your heart, which must beat to keep you alive. It is important to have a healthy heart spiritually, as well. If you mentally and physically exercise your heart muscle, you will find it easier to get through stressful times. A key ingredient is faith and connecting to Hashem. A person with faith tries not to let the daily stresses of life impact him. Through challenging times, always maintain a positive outlook.[115] Even if you are not feeling up to it, maintain a favorable outward appearance. Optimism is contagious! People gravitate to others with a vibrant outlook on life. The opposite is also true. A bitter, angry person causes others to flee, because they carry with them a negative attitude that others can feel. It's best to maintain a safe distance from others who are morally corrupt, because it can be contagious, damaging your faith and draining your energy. If you are having a hard time, please confide in a Rabbi or a friend who will refuel your positivity. Speak to others who were in a similar situation. Optimism, faith, and prayer recharge "The Energy of the Heart" and will ignite the energy of the soul.

Love, Daddy

THE MAIN ENTRANCE

"Competition is an opportunity to become creative."

My Dear Children,

In order to be successful, you must focus on your goals, whether they be physical or spiritual. Please use your G-d given talents to search for your area of interest. Once you've found it, you can select your profession. If you like your profession you will be energized, but if you realize it's not what you want to do with your life, it can become very draining. If, while you're feeling blue, you see others who are thriving, please don't be jealous. Envy is rotten to the core and can make a person miserable. An envious person lacks faith in Hashem and is not grateful for the gifts bestowed upon him.[116] However, there is a healthy form of envy. Imitating other's successful ways is a form of admiration. As they say, imitation is the sincerest form of flattery. Always be happy for others, and Hashem will be happy for you. Others will want to be your friend, because your intentions are selfless, and you want to help others. Competition is not a bad character trait. In business, or in any area of life, competition is an opportunity for growth. It gives you the drive to work harder and succeed. However, if you're competing with someone for the same job, and he is hired, don't begrudge him his success. Spiritually, it's fine to admire another's connection to Hashem. Staying connected with faith and love for your neighbor is "The Main Entrance" into the house of Hashem.

Love, Daddy

KIDS IN ACTION

"Success is created when we are busy, resilient, happy, and cry out to Hashem in prayer."

My Dear Children,

My fondest wish is that you have many children who you can love, appreciate, and cherish. It is man's true wealth. Appreciating the moments of their growth is a miracle. Hashem, in His wisdom, created a baby's growth in stages. If a child was created with all its needs met, the love wouldn't last, since love is about giving and catering to their needs. Human nature needs something to look forward to and anticipating your child's stages of growth is one of life's greatest pleasures. Also, you can learn from children. **Children are always busy.** From this, you can learn to constantly maintain an occupied mind. **Children are resilient!** If they fall or get hurt, they always pick themselves up and move on to their next activity. This can educate you to do the same. If something doesn't go as planned, brush yourself off and keep on going. **Children are always happy and smiling.** Since a child is born with a pure mind, free of the clutter of everyday life, we can learn the value of happiness by appreciating and thanking Hashem for the gifts He is constantly showering us with. **Children cry when they want something!** When you need assistance, cry to Hashem in prayer.[117] This causes an everlasting connection. It creates a bond of faith and trust in a loving Father who will always take care of you. Please never let adulthood rob you of being a "Kid in Action."

Love, Daddy

THE ART OF GIVING

"When helping others, we are actually helping ourselves."

My Dear Children,

The most important thing I learned in life is the art of giving.[118] It is a most admirable trait, and often leads to gaining mentally, physically, financially, and spiritually. When someone comes to you for assistance, try your best to help. It is not always about money; it can just be for moral support or for your time and attention. Giving is the template that built our wonderful nation and community. Sometimes, others may not be as giving. There will be times you will over-extend yourself financially or offer advice and the person may not express his gratitude. Remember, Hashem is in charge! Please don't let it discourage you. Everyone has character flaws. When offering advice, reassure the person you're hoping that Hashem will take care of him and everything will be okay. There will be times you may not reap the reward for giving to others. The best advice I can give you is to give to others with no ulterior motive; let Hashem handle your reward. You can also help others by praying for them. Helping others is a reward, especially if your help makes a positive difference in his life. Please remember, the world was built on Hashem's kindness and giving to others. Imitate Hashem and realize the eternal bonds of love for others is created through "The Art of Giving."

Love, Daddy

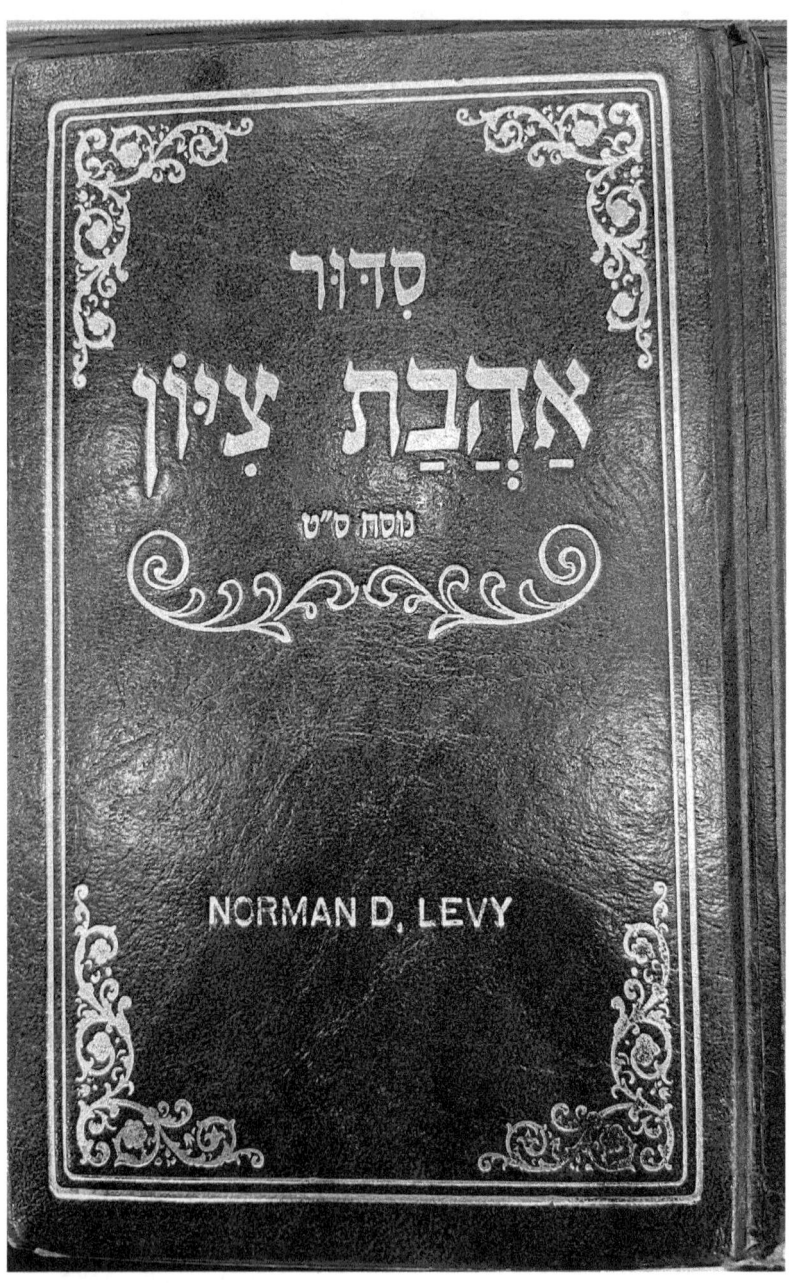

My prayer book.

FINAL THOUGHTS
APPRECIATING HASHEM

Leading our lives on the right path of connecting to Hashem through prayer and appreciation will get us to our destinations. It's not only about appreciating Hashem for the good He sends us, but also about the faith that He knows what He is doing. All we must do is appreciate what we have. Continue to pray and love Hashem with all your heart. That is the greatest blessing. He is our Father that is watching over us and sending miracles every minute of every day.

I thank Hashem for giving me the strength, knowledge, and experience to write this book. My prayer is that this book should serve as a legacy to my children and help anyone seeking or giving advice.

Thank you for taking time to read these words. I hope that they have helped you to remember you are a divine child of Hashem and that you are never forgotten.

May we have the merit to witness the arrival of the Messiah and rebuilding of Jerusalem, in our time. Amen!

ENDNOTES

[1] "And Aharon was silent." (Leviticus/Shemini 10:3)

[2] "And you shall set boundaries for the people." (Exodus/Yitro 19:12)

[3] "And let them make me a sanctuary, that I may dwell among them." (Exodus/Teruma 25:8)

[4] "The Lord, The Lord G-d, Compassionate and Gracious, Slow to Anger and Abundant in Kindness and Truth." (Exodus/Ki Tisa 34:6)

[5] "Blessed are you who forms light and creates darkness." (Morning prayer in prayer book/Yotzer)

[6] "Go into the wilderness and meet Moshe." (Exodus/Shemot 4:27)

[7] "And Noah, the man of the earth, debased himself and planted a vineyard." (Genesis/Noah 9:20)

[8] "You are Standing today before G-d." (Deuteronomy/Nitzavim 29:9)

[9] "They rushed him from the dungeon, he shaved and changed his clothes." (Genesis/Mikeitz 41:14)

[10] "Praise Hashem is His holy place, praise Him in His mighty heavens." (Psalms 150:1)

[11] "Hashem said to Abraham, go for Yourself from your land." (Genesis/Lech Lecha 12:1)

[12] "You shall surely send away the mother and take the young for yourself." (Deuteronomy/Ki Tetzeh 22:7)

[13] "Do not fear and do not be dismayed." (Deuteronomy 1:21)

[14] "May Hashem lift his face for you and establish peace for you." (Numbers/Nasso 6:26)

[15] "Remember what Amalek did to you, on the way, when you were leaving Egypt." (Deuteronomy/Ki Teitzei 25:17)

[16] "Blessed are you, G-d who resurrects the dead." (Second Blessing of the Amidah)

[17] "Blessed Our G-d, who gives the heart understanding to distinguish between day and night" (Morning blessings in prayer book/Birchot Hashachar)

[18] "He brings out prisoners at appropriate times." (Psalms 68:7)

[19] "Blessed art thou Our G-d, who opens the eyes of the blind." (Morning Blessings in prayer book/Birchot Hashachar)

[20] "Blessed are you, G-d who clothes the naked." (Morning Blessings in prayer book/Birchot Hashachar)

[21] "G-d heard their groaning and remembered His covenant with Abraham, Yitchak and Yaacov." (Exodus 2:24)

[22] "He will be like a tree deeply rooted alongside brooks of water." (Psalms 1:3)

[23] "It is from Hashem that a man's footsteps are established." (Psalms 37:23)

[24] "Hope to Hashem, be strong and He will give you courage, and hope to Hashem." (Psalms 27:14)

[25] "Blessed are you G-d, who provides me with all my needs". (Morning Blessings in

prayer book/ Birchot Hashachar)

[26] "Be strong and courageous! Do not be afraid and do not be broken before them." (Deuteronomy/Vayeilech 31:6)

[27] "He leads the humble in the just way and teaches the humble His way." (Psalms 25:9)

[28] "And I will make you a great nation." (Genesis/Lech Lecha 12:2)

[29] "Who is rich? He who rejoices in his portion." (Ethics of the Father 4:1)

[30] "Moshe grew up and went out to his brethren and observed their burdens." (Exodus 2:11)

[31] "A Woman of Valor, who can find- for her price is beyond pearls." (Proverbs 31:10)

[32] "Blessed O' G-d, who has formed man in His wisdom." (Blessings after leaving restroom)

[33] "A song of Ascents, from the depths, I called you, Hashem." (Psalms 130:1)

[34] "My G-d, guard my tongue from evil and my lips from speaking falsehood." (Final paragraph of the Amidah)

[35] "The one who remembers the kindness of our forefathers." (First blessing of Amidah)

[36] "Love your neighbor as you love yourself." (Leviticus/Kedoshim 19:18)

[37] "In His goodness, He constantly renews, every day the act of creation." (Morning prayers in prayer book/Yotzer)

[38] "Provide yourself with a teacher, get yourself a friend and judge them all favorably." (Ethics of the fathers 1:6)

[39] "Train a child according to his way; even when he is old, he will not depart from it." (Proverbs 22:6)

[40] "Master of the universe, I forgive anyone who angered me or antagonized me or sinned against me." (Prayer before Bedtime)

[41] "Only through personal repentance and self-cleansing can a person receive Hashem's forgiveness." (Sforno)

[42] "Let Israel hope for Hashem, for with Hashem is kindness, and with Him is abundant redemption." (Psalms 130:7)

[43] "May Hashem answer you on the day of distress." (Psalms 20:2)

[44] "All of them together gave thanks and acknowledged Your sovereignty." (Prayer before the Amida in prayer book)

[45] "It is Hashem who gives you the power to become prosperous." (Deuteronomy/Ekev 8:18)

[46] "Judges and officers, shall you appoint in all your cities." (Deuteronomy/Shoftim 16:18)

[47] "May you see children born to your children." (Psalms 128:6)

[48] "Desire, Jealousy and pursuit of honor remove a person from the world." (Ethics of the fathers 4:22)

[49] "Your children shall be like olive shoots surrounding your table." (Psalms 128:3)

[50] "Make the offspring of David, your servant, sprout forth quickly." (Amidah Prayer in prayer book)

[51] "I am G-d, your healer." (Exodus/Beshalach 15:26)

[52] "Behold, how good and pleasant it is when brothers dwell together in unity." (Psalms133:1)

[53] "Why do you cry out to me? Speak to the Children of Israel and journey forth." (Exodus/Beshalach 14:15)

[54] "Vanities of Vanities, all is Vanity." (Ecclesiastes 1:2)

[55] "May the expressions of my mouth and the thoughts of my heart find favor before you, Hashem, my rock and my redeemer." (End of Amidah in prayer book)

[56] "So Abraham hastened to the tent to Sarah and said; "Hurry!! Three se'ahs of meal, fine flour! Knead and make cakes." (Genesis/Vayeira 18:6)

[57] "The entire people responded together and said, everything that Hashem has spoken we shall do." (Exodus/Yitro 19:8)

[58] "And you shall teach them thoroughly to your children." (Devarim /Vaetchanan 6:7)

[59] "Then G-d opened her eyes and she perceived a well of water." (Genesis/Vayera 21:19)

[60] "The scepter shall not depart from Judah." (Genesis/Vayechi 49:10)

[61] "Hashem would speak to Moshe, Face to Face." (Exodus/Ki Tisa 33:11)

[62] "May Hashem lift His face to you and establish peace for you." (Numbers/Naso 6:26)

[63] "You shall love Hashem, your G-d, with all your heart, with all your soul, and with all of your resources." (Deuteronomy/Vaetchanan 6:5)

[64] "And it was – just as she coaxed Yosef day after day, and he would not listen to her." (Genesis/Vayeshev 39:10)

[65] "Praiseworthy is the man that walks not in the counsel of the wicked and stood in the path of the sinful." (Psalms1:1)

[66] "The end of all matter, all having been heard: Fear G-d and keep His commandments, for this is a whole man." (Ecclesiastes 12:13)

[67] "He planted an Eshel in Beer-Sheba." (Genesis/Vayera 21:33)

[68] "Surely, if you improve yourself, you will be forgiven. But if you do not improve yourself, sin rests at the door." (Genesis 4:7)

[69] "Blessed are you Hashem, King of the universe, who bestows goodness upon the guilty, who has bestowed goodness upon me." (Blessing of Gratitude)

[70] "Fire and hail, snow and vapor, stormy wind fulfilling his word." (Psalms148:8)

[71] "And Hashem said, I have forgiven because of your word." (Numbers/Shelach 14:20)

[72] "Do not lose it from your lips, or from your children's lips, or your grandchildren's lips." (Morning prayer in prayer book/Ubah Letzion)

[73] "He remembers the kindness of the forefathers and brings redemption to their children's children." (Amida first blessing)

[74] "Six days shall you work and accomplish all of your work, but the seventh day is

Sabbath to Hashem, your G-d." (Exodus/Yitro 20:9)

[75] "I admit before you, everlasting king, that you have returned my soul to me." (First blessing upon awakening in the morning/Elokay Neshama)

[76] "Cast upon Hashem your burden and He will sustain you." (Psalms 55:23)

[77] "And whatever You will give me, I shall repeatedly tithe it to you." (Genesis/Vayetzeh 28:22)

[78] "And give our hearts the understanding to learn and to teach others." (Morning prayers in prayer book/Ahavat Olam)

[79] "My G-d, save me from Evil Speech." (Last blessing of Amida)

[80] "Turn from evil and do good." (Psalms 34:15)

[81] "A broken heart and humbled, O' G-d you will not despise." (Psalms 51:19)

[82] "And G-d said, Let the earth sprout vegetation." (Genesis 1:11)

[83] "You open your hand and satisfy the desire of every living thing." (Psalms145:16)

[84] "All my limbs will say, Hashem, who is like you." (Tehilim 35:10)

[85] "Judah recognized: and he said, she is right, it is from me." (Genesis/Vayeshev 38:26)

[86] "Jacob was left alone, and a man wrestled with him until the break of dawn." (Genesis Vayishlach 32:25)

[87] "He who gives snow like fleece, He scatters frost like ashes." (Psalms 148:16)

[88] "So that you will fear Hashem, your G-d to observe His decrees." (Deuteronomy/Vaetchanan 6:2)

[89] "I shall take you out of the burdens of Egypt; I shall rescue you from their service; I shall redeem you with an outstretched arm; I shall take you to me for a people." (Exodus/Va'era 6:6-7)

[90] "Give thanks to Hashem, for he is good, for His kindness endures forever." (Psalms 107:1)

[91] "Behold now, I desired to speak to my lord although I am but dust and ash." (Genesis/Lech Lecha 18:27)

[92] "And G-d said, Behold I have given you all the herbage yielding seed that is on the surface of the entire earth, and every tree that has seed yielding fruit, it shall be yours for food." (Genesis 1:29)

[93] "He sent Yehuda ahead of him to Yosef, to prepare ahead of him in Goshen." (Genesis/Vayigash 46:28)

[94] "Behold it is a nation that will dwell in solitude." (Numbers/Balak 23:9)

[95] "It happened that when Moshe raised his hand, Israel grew stronger, and when he lowered his hand, Amalek was stronger." (Exodus/Beshalach 17:11)

[96] "I have created the evil one and also created the Torah as its antidote." (Path of the Just)

[97] "And you shall not bring an abomination into your home." (Deuteronomy/Ekev 7:26)

[98] "And you do not turn away from any of the words that I command you this day." (Deuteronomy 28:14)

[99] "He will be like a tree deeply rooted alongside brooks of water." (Psalms 1:3)

[100] "I am Joseph, Is my father still alive." (Genesis 45:3)

[101] "The land that we passed through, to spy out- the Land is very good." (Numbers/ Shelach 14:7)

[102] "Although you intended me harm, G-d intended it for good." (Genesis Vayehi 50:20)

[103] "Give thanks to Hashem, for He is good, for His kindness endures forever." (Psalms 136:1)

[104] "Jonathan again adjured David because of his love for him." (Samuel 1:17)

[105] "Then the spirit of their father Jacob was revived." (Genises/Vayigash 45:27)

[106] "I implored Hashem at that time, saying you have begun to show your servant Your greatness and Your strong arm. (Deuteronomy/Vaetchanan 3:23-24)

[107] "He cried out to Hashem, and Hashem showed him a tree; he threw it into the water and the water became sweet." (Exodus/Beshalach 15:25)

[108] "Hashem descended in a cloud and stood with him there." (Exodus/Ki Tisa 34:5)

[109] "You shall not eat of their flesh, nor shall you touch their carcass- they are unclean to you." (Leviticus/Shemini 11:8)

[110] "It happened that when Moses raised his hand, Israel was stronger, and when he lowered his hand, Amalek was stronger." (Exodus/Beshalach 17:12)

[111] "The sorcerers said to Pharoah, "It is the finger of G-d."(Exodus/Va'era 8:15)

[112] "Be of the disciples of Aaron, loving peace, pursuing peace." (Ethics of the Fathers 1:12)

[113] "Never again has there arisen in Israel a prophet like Moses, whom Hashem knew face to face." (Deuteronomy/Vezot Haberacha 34:10)

[114] "Your right hand, Hashem, is glorified with strength, your right hand, Hashem, smashes the enemy." (Exodus/Beschalach 15:6)

[115] "Hashem was with Joseph, and He endowed him with charisma." (Genesis 39:21)

[116] "You shall not covet your fellow's wife, his man servant, his maid servant, his ox, his donkey, or anything that belongs to your fellow." (Exodus/Yitro 20:14)

[117] "My voice is to G-d, when I cry, My voice is to G-d, please listen to me." (Psalms 77:2)

[118] "For, I said, Forever will Your kindness be built." (Psalms 89:3)

ABOUT THE AUTHOR

Norman D. Levy is an entrepreneur who has been selling in the garment industry for the past 30 years. His sales career started with his cousin and he gravitated into retail, where he worked successfully with his father for 7 years. He is also an avid writer having been published in various publications and magazines. This is his first book.

Norman's greatest wish is to assist others as others have helped him. He is strong in his faith and hopes that all those who are struggling find their way back Home to Hashem.

Norman lives in New Jersey with his wife and children. He is a proud father and grandfather and enjoys spending quality time with his family. On a daily basis, Norman enjoys going to synagogue where he learns and prays. In his spare time, he enjoys going to the gym, bicycle riding and playing tennis.

ACKNOWLEDGMENTS

This book is dedicated in loving memory to my father David Nissim Levy. He was a man that dedicated his life for his wife and children. It was my father's common-sense training that was a seed to my personal and professional accomplishments.

This book is in honor of my wife, Lauren, and all my children, who have been a constant inspiration to help me write this book.

In addition, I want to thank my mother, Marie Levy, and my sisters, Vicki Grazi, Michelle Tobias, and Jacqueline Chabot, for always being there as a support system for myself and my children.

I would like to thank the following people for their constant help and guidance to make this book a reality.

Norman S. Levy ᴬ"ᴴ - My cousin and mentor. Norman was the first to notice my passion for writing.

Jacob S. Kassin - For close to 30 years, Jacob's door has always been open to me. Jacob spent countless hours assisting me with ideas on the format and layout of this book. His guidance and experience helped me speed up this project into a reality.

Rabbi David Ozery - My Rabbi that has been there for me until this very day. There was always a place for me in his home, where I became very close to his sons and was treated closer than a family member. We are very close and he has led me through my journeys with sincerity and support.

Rabbi David Sutton - I listen to Rabbi Sutton's classes daily. He wrote a few books that I cherish. I thank him for his daily infusion of knowledge.

Rabbi Duvi Ben Soussan - The Rabbi spent countless hours guiding me and helping me through my most challenging times.

Rabbi Michael Haber - Rabbi Haber has always been there for me. He used to visit my dad regularly and always gave me the best advice. I adapted much of my writing styles, based on his eloquent way of speaking.

Rabbi Eli J. Mansour - I love and relate very well to his classes. Listening to his classes online, assisted me tremendously with my spiritual growth.

Rabbi David Nahem - Rabbi Nahem invested a lot of time in my spiritual journey. We spent many hours discussing my challenges and his advice was always perfect!

Rabbi Moshe Malka - Rabbi Malka is a phone call away and always there for us. His dedicated service to our community is unparalleled.

Rabbi Ricky Cohen - Over 20 years ago, Ricky suggested that I start writing for *Jewish Image Magazine*, our community magazine. I always had a place in his heart and a place setting in his home, whenever I wanted to come for Shabbat/Holidays. My family is forever grateful.

Michael Jemal - A great cousin and friend. We have been friends since we were toddlers. At every chapter in this book, Michael was always there to make sure I was in good hands. Michael was responsible for bringing me to Yad Yosef Torah Center, where I started my religious growth.

David J. Beyda - David was always there for me whenever I needed to talk. We have been friends for 42 years. I never had a brother, but I consider David my brother.

Ike Escava - My childhood friend, always there for me. He demonstrates what a true friend should be.

Gabe Zeitouni - Gabe and I became friends when we were 14 years old. He has always been there for advice whenever I needed to talk.

Sammy J. Sutton - During my challenging times, every Friday my phone would ring. "Where are you for dinner tonight? How was your week? How is work?" Totally unconditional selflessness from a great friend.

Yad Yosef Torah Center - The synagogue where I found myself again. Being greeted with warmth and love from childhood friends (too many to mention) and family was a contributing factor to help me write this book.

Carlos Zalta - Like a brother, he has always been there for me and my children whenever needed. A genuine character!

Ronny Grazi - A selfless, kind person who has demonstrated sterling traits in my journey. I am blessed that he is my son David's father-in-law.

Elliot Braha - I met Elliot in Rabbi Mansour's classes and his friendship and guidance was a great inspiration to my religious growth.

Morris Sutton - A cousin and a great friend who was always there for me. A selfless kindhearted person.

Jack Hazan - Jack has been a great friend that was always there for me. His house was always open to me for Shabbat/Holidays.

Harry Adjmi - At a moment's notice, Harry has always been there to advise me in business. His advice has helped me with my career tremendously.

Elliot Tawil - Elliot is a great friend that is always there for me. His "common sense" approach to life is very precious to me.

Steven Bissu^AH - Steven used to read my articles in *Jewish Image Magazine* and suggested I write a book.

Renee Beyda - Renee was very involved in working on this project with me. We spent hours on ideas to develop this book.

Karen Tovsky - Karen is an editor for *Jewish Image Magazine* and loved my articles. When I decided to publish the book, she worked for *Jewish Image Magazine* and edited most of the book for me.

Ben Gurion and Rochelle Matsas - As owners of *Jewish Image Magazine*, they published over 100 of my articles, which served as a guiding point to write this book.

Jeffrey Sitt - Jeff loved my idea for the book and introduced me to Fay Thompson, who put the finishing touches on the editing.

Fay Thompson - Fay worked on the final editing and layout of the book for publishing, a wonderful person to work with.

Joseph Rishty - Joey has been publishing my work in weekly bulletins distributed among our community synagogues.

Rabbi Moshe Shamah - During my formative High School years at Sephardic High School, he always displayed confidence in me. He knew all of his students individually and formed a school of unity.

Rabbi Ronald Barry - He ran Sephardic High School from the background and his door was always open for me. He is a great man with an open heart to all.

It is a great asset to be blessed with close friends and Rabbis. I am blessed with many friends that have always been in my corner. Through each highway and byway, they have been there for me to rebuild my personal and spiritual lifestyle.

This work would not be a reality if it wasn't for my dear Rabbis. Receiving a daily education from my Rabbis developed my spirituality to write this work. When I started to get close to the Rabbis of our community, it was transparent that Hashem is loving and is guiding our steps on a minute-to-minute basis.